# THE FIVE SECRETS OF LUCK

## A Tale of the Long-Lost Keys to an Extraordinary Life

# SKIP JOHNSON

# THE FIVE SECRETS OF LUCK

## A Tale of the Long-Lost Keys to an Extraordinary Life

# SKIP JOHNSON

Copyright © 2025 Skip Johnson

All rights reserved. No part of this book may be reproduced or transmitted in any form or by any means, electronic or mechanical, including photocopying, recording, or by any information storage and retrieval system without written permission of the publisher, except for the inclusion of brief quotations in a review. This is a work of fiction.

Cover and Interior Design by Dino Marino | dinomarinodesign.com

Copy Editing by Jessica Andersen | jessicalandersen.com

Proofreading by Linda Dutro | lindadutro@gmail.com

Paperback ISBN: 979-8-218-83293-3

eBook ISBN: 979-8-9871654-9-2

"Luck is the residue of design."

–Branch Rickey

# Acknowledgments

Thank you as always to my extraordinary team that helped bring yet another project together: Editor Jessica Andersen, Proofreader Linda Dutro, Cover Designer and Interior Format Specialist Dino Marino, and Web Designer Emily Grimaldi.

I also want to say thanks to my brother-in-law, Doctor Eric Sewell, and my friend Philip Nelson for their wise counsel in developing this story.

Additionally, I'm grateful once again to my Advance Review Team. Launching is critical to a book's success, and your work helps ensure each novel I write reaches more and more readers around the world. Thank you!

# OTHER BOOKS
# BY SKIP JOHNSON

All books available at www.skipjohnsonauthor.com

### *The Mystic's Gift:*
### *A Story About Loss, Letting Go . . .*
### *and Learning to Soar*

*(Book 1 in The Mystic's Gift/Royce Holloway series)*

A spellbinding, deeply moving story that is quickly becoming a self-help classic. Following a sudden, unimaginable personal tragedy at a point in his midlife when Royce Holloway thought he had it all, he is introduced to a wise, exotic, enchanting mentor named Maya, who takes Royce on a powerful journey of courageous self-discovery and incredible possibilities.

What he learns on this captivating, often poignant trek across two continents will change him in a powerful way, but you may find that the life changed most . . . is yours.

### *The Gentleman's Journey:*
### *A Heartwarming Story of Courage,*
### *Compassion, and Wisdom*

*(Book 2 in The Mystic's Gift/Royce Holloway series)*

Five years after that glorious week when Maya shared six life-changing principles from an ancient secret book of wisdom with him, Royce is ready for a new chapter—to push his skills and his life to a higher level and make an even greater impact on the world.

In fact, he feels something is *leading* him to do that very thing . . .

So much so, that when Royce's journey takes him to the spectacular, historical Jekyll Island Club Hotel on the Georgia coast, it doesn't surprise him one bit when he "coincidentally" meets a mysterious, well-seasoned world traveler, a traveler whose life was *destined* to intersect with Royce Holloway's—in an unforgettable way for them both.

Join Royce on this powerful, spellbinding trek full of mystics, miracles, and inspirational stories.

You may find *your* life will never be the same again . . .

### *The Treasure in Antigua*

*(Book 3 in The Mystic's Gift/Royce Holloway series)*

When Royce Holloway ends up on the magnificent island of Antigua, it's far from a Caribbean vacation. Instead, he finds himself on an incredible journey to locate a sacred, priceless treasure—one that Godfrey Tillman said would deeply impact Royce—and deeply impact the world.

*If* the carefully hidden prize could ever be found . . .

Along the way, Royce is led through a series of "co-incidental" meetings with wise, inspirational mentors from all walks of life, who somehow seem part of a mysterious, bigger plan to guide him in reaching his destination.

Join Royce on his captivating, empowering, and often poignant trek across beautiful Antigua, and as you meet the different teachers on his path, you'll likely find the "student" whose life is changed most . . . is you.

### *The Lottery Winner's Greatest Ride:*
### *A Millionaire, a Young Reporter . . .*
### *and a Journey to Find What Matters Most*

When Phillip Westford won the biggest lottery in history, he never dreamed there would be a price to pay.

A very *large* price that would shake his world to the core . . .

But just when he is at his breaking point, Phillip meets a mysterious old Irishman named Patrick O'Rourke who claims he knows the secret for getting the distraught young man back to happiness.

That is, *if* Phillip is willing to undertake a trek to find three wise mentors across the globe.

Join Phillip on a magnificent train ride as he shares the inspiring, incredible story of his journey of transformation with Juliette McKelvey, a young journalist who is on her own desperate journey to rebuild her crumbling life.

It's a ride to happiness you'll soon realize . . . you were *destined* to be on.

### *The Statue's Secret:*
### *The Answers We Seek Can Often Be Found*
### *In The Most Unlikely Places*

Prominent Newport lawyer David Langley is a tormented man consumed by anxiety, guilt, and regret as his world falls apart more and more each day.

Until . . .

He fortuitously comes across an ancient Caribbean statue, which is soon verified as one of the most magnificent, sacred artifacts ever unearthed.

A relic that had a unique blessing bestowed upon it for the benefit of its fourteenth-century owner—and for all future owners . . .

A blessing that it seems could finally lead David on a path to a transformed life.

That is, *if* David can find his way to a mystical meeting with three wise, carefully chosen mentors at a remote location deep within the Dominican Republic jungle . . . within 48 hours.

Otherwise, the statue and its remarkable gift will vanish forever.

As David frantically, desperately makes his way to his final Dominican destination and the opportunity for an inspired new life, you'll find yourself enthusiastically cheering him on every step of the way.

Then, at some point you may realize the one who is truly on the journey . . . is *you*.

### *The Cobbler of Cape Town:*
### *A Tale of Courage, Love, and Transformation*

In the 1930s, years before South Africa's famous freedom movement began, a humble, wise cobbler named Eli was dreaming of happiness in Cape Town.

It was a bold dream about prosperity for everyone in his divided land—not just the privileged few.

At the same time, a distraught yet determined eighteen-year-old named Lucas arrived in Cape Town from Holland on what he hoped would be a transformative, healing journey of service after suffering a family tragedy.

When destiny brings the pair together, Eli and Lucas make a divinely inspired pact to lay the groundwork for empowerment and hope for the oppressed people.

With The Cobbler's Creed as their sacred compass, the men embark on the impossible task of bringing happiness and belief to Cape Town . . .

But the ruthless, separative South African government learns of their progress, and the politicians begin fearing the ever-growing influence of the two men, vowing to stop them at any cost.

With their lives in danger and time running out, Eli and Lucas find themselves facing adversity that tests every ounce of their strength and courage.

Set in the enchanting, awe-inspiring African landscape, The Cobbler of Cape Town is a gripping tale and an inspirational guide for those on a pilgrimage to overcome fear, doubt, and heartache—and make the world a better place.

### *The Innkeeper's Journal:*
### *A Tale of Self-Discovery*

Set in a picturesque town on the Georgia coast, it's the story of a wealthy, entitled young couple from Boston, Nick and Maggie Reynolds, who are struggling through a relationship that seems headed for a bitter divorce.

Then, on a road trip to Florida, in a final, desperate attempt to rekindle their formerly fairy-tale marriage, they fortuitously take a detour that could change everything . . .

Stopping at a quaint bed and breakfast on the island of St. Simons, the pair meets the kind, jovial, yet mysterious coastal innkeeper Vince van Note.

It's Vince who soon introduces them to a powerful set of secretive, life-enhancing principles called The Four Truths, written in a journal by one of the most famous painters in history, over a hundred years ago.

When the innkeeper sends Maggie and Nick on daily "assignments" across the island to seek out magnificent manifestations of The Four Truths all around them, their eyes began opening to the unimaginable possibilities . . .

They start to understand how a life of greater peace, appreciation, joy, compassion, and love may have been available to them all along.

If they had only known The Four Truths . . .

Join Nick and Maggie as they take a life-changing journey through the spectacular Golden Isles of Georgia, frantically trying to recover true happiness and love for each other.

### *Hidden Jewels of Happiness:*
### *Powerful Essays for Finding and Savoring*
### *the Gifts on Your Journey*

A book of wisdom, encouragement, and empowerment for dealing with life's daily challenges. Let Skip reveal to you the seemingly hidden gifts that are all around us, waiting to be discovered and savored. You'll feel inspired, enlightened, and happier with every page.

### *Grateful for Everything:*
### *Learning, Living, and Loving*
### *the Great Game of Life*

A deeply engaging book that provides a blueprint for using the power of gratitude to increase your happiness and fulfillment. You'll find delightful stories and practical ideas for turning your life into a great game to play each day, instead of a dreary battle to be fought.

# Table Of Contents

# Chapter One

Christopher Stone felt like the unluckiest man in the world.

Squinting through the rain falling in sheets, he clamped down on the steering wheel, desperately looking for his exit. He and his wife, Sarah, had driven this stretch of interstate for what seemed like hundreds of times as they headed east to their favorite inn on the border of Georgia and Tennessee.

But this time, she wasn't his copilot—and she likely never would be again.

The forty-five-year-old business owner blinked rapidly as if to clear his vision, but also as if he were trying to clear his thoughts from the past five miserable years. The bitter divorce felt like confirmation everything in his life was utterly . . . awful.

Finally, he spotted the sign for Lookout Mountain, a town just a few miles outside of Chattanooga. As he steadily guided the car toward the exit, his eyes welled up, remembering past trips to the Magnolia Inn at the top of the mountain.

"Aren't we lucky?" Sarah would beam each time the couple reached this point on their trip. "Here we are, once again getting to spend a week enjoying Southern hospitality at our favorite little inn."

But that was then, and the solo traveler certainly didn't feel *lucky* now.

Although the clouds were beginning to lift and the rain was finally letting up, the conditions in his head weren't improving. Christopher still couldn't wrap his brain around how much had gone wrong in such a short period of time. His marriage had collapsed, the business had struggled, he had a horrible accident, and he had become estranged from his precious daughter, Megan.

Then there were the chest pains he kept ignoring . . .

Christopher's thoughts abruptly halted as he spied a stretch of road leading up the mountain. Once off the Tennessee interstate, he had driven through the outskirts of Chattanooga but barely even registered those ten minutes. He was relieved to have reached the final leg of his journey after having left New Mexico twelve hours before.

As the car crept along the snaky mountain lane, he glanced at the valley below becoming smaller and smaller.

Maybe, just maybe, he could leave everything behind for the long weekend—the intense loneliness, the bitterness, the deep sadness. Nothing else had worked, so his therapist had suggested the road trip, although Christopher was doubtful about the journey's potential to heal him.

At last, he reached the top and saw the familiar MAGNOLIA INN sign at the first intersection. He turned the car to the left, made another quick turn into the pebble driveway, and then steered his car snuggly into the first parking space he found, right across from the inn's office entrance.

"Finally, a stroke of luck," he said aloud with a smirk. "Wonder what the catch is?" He shook his head and sighed. It seemed like only yesterday he felt invincible, but now he couldn't shake the feeling the deck of life was stacked against him.

He stepped out of the car and stretched his arms and legs. It felt like he had been cooped up for days, even though he had stopped frequently on his drive from Albuquerque. He took in the familiar sights of the inn grounds, which he loved so much. The stone façade of the eighteen rooms gave the place a unique look and feel—like something out of Hansel and Gretel, the story he had read as a child.

As he closed the car door, a young woman of about twenty stepped out of the office. "Hi, Mr. Stone! It's been a while . . . haven't seen you and your wife for quite some time!"

"Yeah, we missed last year," he mumbled sheepishly.

She peered at the passenger's side and cocked her head in concern. "Where's Mrs. Stone?"

"Um, she . . . couldn't make it this year. Maybe next year." His gaze dropped, and the receptionist seemed to take the hint.

"Oh, well, I understand. Please give her my regards. In the meantime, let's get you checked in." She smiled softly and walked back into the office, holding the door open for Christopher.

The short, brown-haired woman stepped behind the counter to consult her ledger, then pointed across the parking lot. "You'll be in your usual room—Number 7, right behind the pool."

"Um, great, thanks, Jessica." Christopher grabbed a blue ballpoint pen on the counter and scribbled his name on the registration form. He turned the clipboard back around to the receptionist, who handed him a small brass key.

"Here you go, Mr. Stone."

Christopher mustered a quick smile, took the key, and offered a final "Thanks" before heading back to the car. He inhaled slowly and deeply, then dragged his two red suitcases out of the trunk and began the short walk across the crunchy driveway to Room 7. . .

# CHAPTER TWO

The travel-weary man plopped the suitcases down just outside his room.

He reached in his pocket for the key, then craned his neck to peek in the window through the slightly open curtains. Although the room *looked* the same as usual, he felt a lump rise in his throat as he realized he had never been at the lodge without his wife. Shaking his head to dispel the old memories, he placed the key into the lock. He turned it smoothly and the door opened, revealing the exquisite, antique cherry furniture just as he remembered.

Scanning the space, he saw the colorful paintings of the jagged Smoky Mountains on two opposing walls, and a gold-framed lithograph of downtown Lookout Mountain, likely from the early 1920's, on another wall. His gaze lingered on the black-and-white image. *Life must have been so simple back then. Friendly people, short business hours, happy families, just . . . simple.*

Christopher exhaled slowly, then hauled his suitcases over the threshold. The larger one he put on the luggage stand and unzipped, but the smaller suitcase he set in the corner on the other side of the room, habitually tucking it out of the way to make sure his wife had plenty of space for her own items.

*Idiot*, he told himself. *She's not here.* He turned back to close the door he had inadvertently left open, and as he stepped toward it, his gaze fell to the floor at a small flyer, which he scooped up with curiosity.

Christopher squinted at the paper, which read: LOOKOUT MOUNTAIN COFFEE SHOP. *Hmmm, that sounds like something I could use right now.* He glanced at his watch and, noting that it was only four thirty, decided to take a quick walk to check it out since he had never been there before.

He set the flyer on the nightstand and went back to his open suitcase to pull out a pair of khaki shorts and a navy T-shirt with NEW MEXICO blazed across the front. Slipping out of his slacks and his wrinkled, white button-down, he quickly donned the casual, cooler attire for the hot local weather.

Throwing on a pair of flip flops, Christopher grabbed his keys and stepped outside, seeing the sun was starting to make an appearance. *Might as well walk, I've got plenty of time*, he told himself. He locked up, crossed the parking lot, and turned left towards downtown Lookout Mountain.

As he strolled along the narrow sidewalk, Christopher noted all the old, knee-high stone walls in front of the homes, in typical Lookout Mountain fashion. He glanced up at the street signs and was quickly reminded that most of them were named after characters from classic stories. Cinderella Road, Red Riding Hood Trail, Peter Pan Drive . . . Sarah had loved this about the little town. "I feel like I'm in a fairy tale," she'd say. Christopher would chuckle and reply, "Well, you're *my* princess." She never seemed to tire of hearing those words, and he never tired of saying them.

He continued to daydream about the trips the two had made over the years. They had connected with so many people in Lookout Mountain, including the previous innkeepers, and he had assumed he and Sarah would always have "their" place together in the charming little mountain town.

But Christopher pushed that thought out of his mind as he continued down the sidewalk. Ahead he saw one of the quaint wooden-arrow signs pointing to downtown, and he realized it was only about a quarter of a mile away. He picked up his pace—partly to get a little more exercise, but mostly to get to his destination quickly and perhaps escape the creeping nostalgia.

On the way, majestic oak trees and river birches lined so many of the streets. He loved Lookout Mountain's tradition of placing flags along the roads during the American flag holidays, which were often when Christopher and Sarah had visited the community together. The flags were out today, even though it was two weeks until the Fourth of July weekend. Nevertheless, the ritual comforted Christopher and brought a smile to his face.

He soon reached the downtown area, which was as quaint as ever. There was only a small strip of shops, all impeccably landscaped, and the shopping center was directly across from a gorgeous red brick Baptist church. The white steeple seemed to fill the brightening sky, and with the manicured emerald fescue surrounding it, the colors were a welcome delight to his dull feelings. Christopher took it all in as he strolled closer to the coffee shop, eventually spotting its small, red shingle jutting out over the glass door.

Pushing the door gently open, he was greeted by the aroma of freshly brewed coffee wafting through the shop from the back. The place was empty of other patrons, but Christopher glanced at his watch and noted that it was now just before five o'clock.

The young barista with long, dark hair held back in a red bandana flashed a smile at the visitor.

"Still open?" Christopher asked.

"Yep, for about another hour—and I'm brewing a fresh pot now if you're interested."

Christopher nodded. "Very interested. I'll take a large, please."

"You got it."

As the barista turned away, Christopher scanned the shop. There were eight small tables along the left wall, three booths on the right side, and two inviting sofas in the center. "Bet Sarah would like this place," he mumbled.

The barista whirled around. "Sir?"

"Oh, nothing, just . . . nothing."

At that moment the front door opened, and a muscular, red-haired man in a fitted, short sleeve madras shirt walked in with his golden retriever. As he approached the counter, he nodded at Christopher, who reciprocated.

Right then, something shiny dropped from the pocket of the man's faded jeans.

Instinctively, Christopher bent down and picked it up. It was a silver keychain shaped like a four-leaf clover, with two keys attached and an inscription on the back.

Christopher handed the charm back to the man, whose hand was outstretched in anticipation.

"Thanks. I'm Lucky."

Christopher laughed. "Of course you are. With a keychain like that, there's no doubt about it. At least *one* of us in here is lucky."

The bearded man, likely around sixty years old, grinned. "No, I mean, my *name* is Lucky. I'm Lou McGraw, and they call me Lucky." He extended his hand in greeting, and the New Mexican clasped it firmly.

"Ah, well, that would *not* be my nickname these days. I'm Christopher Stone."

Lou nodded graciously. "Nice to meet you."

"Lucky Lou . . ." Christopher mused. "I'm sure there's quite a backstory there."

Lou waved his hand in dismissal. "Yeah, but I didn't miss your comment about me being the only lucky one here." He looked around the otherwise empty shop. "What makes you so sure *you're* not lucky, too?" Lou reached down to stroke the soft fur of his four-legged companion and then stared into the weary traveler's eyes.

"If you knew what my life has been like, you wouldn't have to ask. In fact, I bet I'm the *unluckiest* man in this whole state right now. At least, I feel that way."

Lucky raised an eyebrow, cocked his head, and cast a sly grin at the stranger. "You do seem a little unlucky, come to think of it."

Christopher's eyes popped. "Excuse me?"

Lucky calmly continued, "I feel like I'm the *luckiest* man in the state—maybe in the whole country."

Christopher cut his eyes toward the man in annoyance. "Well, good for you."

Lou shrugged nonchalantly. "Just sayin'. . . that's how I feel. But, there's plenty of room for other people in the 'lucky club'—if they're willing to do the work."

Christopher furrowed his brow at the older man.

Right then, the barista broke in, speaking to Christopher. "Here's your coffee, sir. Cream and sugar?"

He shook his head. "Black is fine. Thanks."

The employee nodded. "Coffee's on the house today, gentlemen. It's your lucky day." He grinned at Lou and passed him a steaming cup too.

"Always grateful to be here, Sam. Thanks very much." Lucky held up the cup toward the barista as if he were toasting him.

Turning to Christopher, he inquired, "How long are you in town?"

"Three days, I think."

Lucky nodded, and then his gaze fell to his four-legged friend. "Let's go home, Lep. It's been a good day."

Looking back at Christopher, he added with a wink, "It's a small town, so I'm sure I'll see you around. I think we may be able to get you in the lucky club if you're interested in membership."

With a sarcastic eyeroll, the New Mexican countered, "Well, I would love to join, but *that* would take more than a few days."

Lucky shrugged and smiled. "You never know. See you soon, Christopher."

His words hung in the air as Christopher ran his fingers through his thick salt-and-pepper hair, observing Lucky step outside.

He murmured to the barista, "Odd dude, huh?"

"Lucky? I'd say he's a *wise* dude. His nickname is well deserved. Things just go *right* for him—or at least, that's the way it seems to most folks around here."

Christopher's forehead creased, then he turned back toward the large front window, just in time to see Lucky and Lep disappear around the corner of the red brick building. . . .

# Chapter Three

The walk back to the inn was made a little easier by the freshly brewed coffee, and as he walked, Christopher reflected on his meeting with Lou McGraw. He thought back on the days when *he* had felt lucky, too—business was booming, his daughter loved him unconditionally, and Sarah only had eyes for him.

But it all started crumbling . . . and then, there was no turning back.

Christopher felt tears welling up in his eyes, and he reached to wipe them away. The sequence was happening more and more these days: the memories, the regrets, then the tears. If only he hadn't worked so much. If only he had made more time for his family. If only he hadn't been so selfish. If only his wife understood him better . . .

Just then, a sports car swerved close to the sidewalk, and Christopher felt a rush of air when it sped by. His cup of coffee fell to the ground as he jumped instinctively away from the passing car; then, looking at the drink which was now spilled all over the sidewalk, he shook his head and cursed. *Unlucky one more time. I can't even drink a cup of coffee without a near disaster happening.*

*Then again, maybe that disaster would have been for the best.* Fuming, he marched a few steps over to the empty paper cup and stomped on it.

In ten minutes, Christopher was back at The Magnolia Inn. As he walked onto the pebbled parking lot, voices from the pool carried over to him. He turned and saw happy couples lying in the sun loungers, holding hands and chatting animatedly. It seemed like yesterday that Christopher and Sarah were doing the same. They had loved meeting friends, swapping stories, and laughing together on their trips . . .

At that moment, a feminine voice called from behind him, "Hey, do you know where Room 9 is?"

Christopher turned and saw an attractive, dark-haired woman, maybe five years younger than him, with a shapely figure. She was shrugging her shoulders, and her palms were turned up. "I can't find it, and the receptionist got tied up on the phone as soon as I checked in."

The corners of Christopher's mouth lifted as he pointed two rooms down from his. "Just over there—and you're close to the pool, if you like that kind of thing."

"Thanks. I'm down from Connecticut, and believe it or not, it's still cool up there, so a nice dip might feel good."

"Yeah, the water is *not* chilly. I'm from New Mexico, and it's almost as hot down here in the summer. It's the humidity, I guess."

Her brown eyes twinkled. "Well, the water sounds good. I think I might get changed and head that way in a few minutes."

Christopher nodded. "Maybe I'll see you there tomorrow—it's been a long day of travel for me." He added, "I'm Christopher."

"I'm Madeline. Nice to meet you." She tucked a lock of her wavy, shoulder-length hair behind her ear and smiled as she extended her hand.

Christopher reached out and shook it. "Great to meet you, Madeline. I'll look forward to seeing you around." He turned toward his room as she walked to her car.

Giving the pool a wide berth, Christopher couldn't help but acknowledge how good it felt to just talk with a woman—though it was a brief interaction. Since the divorce, he really hadn't spoken much with women. He had lost so much self-confidence that he no longer wanted to engage in conversation. But being away from New Mexico was already relaxing him, and he smiled, thinking about the quick chat.

Once in his room, Christopher sat on the bed. On the nightstand, the flyer for the coffee shop caught his eye. He remembered the chance meeting with Lucky. What did "the lucky club" even mean? And why did he think Christopher seemed unlucky after talking with him for only a minute? Christopher truly couldn't understand it right now—but he did know he was hungry.

He dialed the number for room service, and a cheerful female voice came on the line. "Hi, Mr. Stone, what can I get you?"

"I'd love a cheeseburger if you happen to have one on the menu."

"Right away, sir. Would you like fries with that?"

"Why not? You only live once." He managed to chuckle, and the woman on the other end laughed too.

"We'll have it to you in about twenty minutes— hope you enjoy, Mr. Stone."

Christopher hung up the phone and relaxed into the bed once more. It was all so odd, ordering for one person, having a room for one . . . all the "single" things. It had been six months since the divorce was finalized, and he had thought the solo life would have felt more routine at this point. *But not for me,* a small voice in his mind insisted.

*"It'll take some time,"* friends had glibly advised.

Christopher reflected on that, too. He hadn't expected to lose friends or to see them "choose sides." In fact, he realized that he hadn't been prepared for *any* of the ripple effects of the divorce. He and Sarah had been a pair since high school, and it never crossed his mind that someday they wouldn't be together anymore.

He heard Sarah had already moved on. She was dating, and it really didn't come as a surprise. She was a lovely woman with a charming personality, so of course men would find her appealing. It just happened so soon after their separation, and to think of it still pained him so much . . .

At that moment, a loud knocking broke the silence. Christopher shook his head to snap out of the sentimental thoughts, then stood and walked toward the door.

"Hi, Mr. Stone," the cheerful young woman said when he opened it. "Here is your, um . . ." Her countenance suddenly changed. "Mr. Stone, are you okay?"

It was then he realized—with a pang of embarrassment—his eyes were moist. He stuttered, "Oh, I, uh . . . must have fallen asleep with my contact lenses in. Probably not the best idea." He managed a half smile, and the woman seemed convinced.

Christopher reached toward the nightstand and grabbed a twenty-dollar bill. "Here you are. Thank you for getting this to me so quickly."

She accepted the cash with gratitude. "Anything else, Mr. Stone?"

"No, but thank you. You're very kind."

Taking the tray with one hand, he closed the door with the other as the girl turned back to the main building.

Christopher switched on the TV to a random program as he gobbled down his dinner. He followed it all with a cold beer he fished out of the mini fridge.

In a way, it felt like his bachelor days, he mused as he sat and stared at the screen. But back then, he was typically getting ready to go see Sarah or take her on a date. Now, he had nowhere to go, and it felt *weird*.

After another hour of mindlessly flipping through shows, Christopher realized it must be nearly nine. He switched off the TV and walked to the bathroom to begin preparing for bed. As he brushed his teeth, he was shocked by how old he looked in the mirror.

"Just one thing after another," he mumbled aloud. "But at least I'm still here . . . for now."

Christopher stepped back into the bedroom, turned down the covers, and eased into bed. *Pathetic,* he thought to himself. *You're still sleeping on "your" side of the bed. As though Sarah were right next to you.* He huffed, turned off the light, and fell sound asleep.

When he awoke the next morning, the groggy traveler pulled back the curtains and saw it was a bright, sunny day on the mountain. He decided to grab a bite of breakfast at the main house, and he briefly debated on whether to exercise afterward. His fitness had suffered like his mental health had in recent years, but he kept kicking the workout can down the road. Today, he decided to kick it a little farther.

Entering the restaurant, he steered clear of the table he usually sat at with Sarah, instead seating himself at a table toward the back near a window. When the server, a young man of about twenty, saw Christopher sit down, he walked over and brought him coffee. "Here you go, sir. No cream or sugar, right?"

"Correct—and how did you know?" asked Christopher, smiling.

"The chef saw you come in. He said it's the way you've always started your day here." He grinned. "He also said you like scrambled eggs, dry wheat toast, and bacon. Is that right?"

Christopher threw back his head and clapped. "Another reason I love this place! You all know exactly what I want—before I even ask!"

The young man smiled and gave a slight bow. "Our pleasure, sir. We'll have that breakfast coming right up."

Christoper nodded his thanks and then turned to look out the window. There was a beautiful view of Chattanooga in the distance, though it certainly wasn't the same without his travel companion. But then he heard a voice, and he turned back to find Madeline standing beside his table.

"Would you like some company this morning? I promise I'm low maintenance." She grinned.

"Sure, that sounds good. But I'll have to warn you, I wake up kind of slow—nothing personal."

"I get that. Lately I've been pushing myself to get up early, since it's just me now. Otherwise, I think I would stay in bed all morning—or all day." She blushed.

Christopher nodded in understanding. "Sounds like you and I may have something in common. Divorce?"

She shook her head. "My husband unexpectedly died a year ago. I've been trying to get used to being on my own, but it's been a struggle. I'm taking this little trip down South as a getaway—and to possibly reconnect with a long-lost friend. Maybe it will all help me regain my sanity."

"I understand. Seems like the harder I try, the worse it gets. I mean, I'm not trying to sound like a whiner, but . . ."

She held up her hand to interrupt. "No, please— I'm the same way. I feel guilty even bringing up Andy's death—and I'm surprised I even said something to you about it."

"My therapist would say you're healing a little if you can do that—so it's a good thing."

She nodded.

The server returned with an extra place setting and asked Madeline what she wanted to start off with.

"Black coffee, please. Also, a glass of orange juice."

"Anything to eat, ma'am?"

"No, thank you." Once the server turned away again, Madeline explained, "Trying to lose a few pounds."

He grinned. "I can relate to that, but . . . if I might say so, you don't look like you need to lose any weight."

She shrugged. "I guess we're our own worst critics."

Christopher nodded, then took a sip of his coffee. "Have any kids?"

The woman shook her head. "Never did. Sometimes I wonder if that was a good thing or not. I mean, it's not like we had any choice in the matter, but . . ."

Christopher broke in gently. "Sounds like you and I are in situations that we never could have predicted." He shrugged. "They say things work out for the best, but I'm not so sure."

Madeline's orange juice and coffee was served, and she took the juice glass and held it up to offer a toast. "To new beginnings, and to trusting there is a better plan for both of us."

Christopher raised his glass.

"Yes, to that!" He grinned, and together, they took a sip of their drinks.

Madeline glanced out the window. "I'm heading for a hike soon, since I'm checking out this afternoon."

Christopher tried to hide his surprise and disappointment. "Leaving town already?"

She nodded and, with a sheepish look, added, "Yes, I was just here for the night. I understand there's so much to see in the South . . . I thought I would keep going."

"Ah, I see. Well, I was hoping we could continue our conversation at the pool a little later today."

Madeline shrugged her shoulders, then her lips turned up gently. "I should be back from my hike after lunch, and I got my checkout delayed until four, so . . . maybe we could catch up at some point."

He smiled in approval. "Sounds good. As for me, this morning I was going to head back up to this local coffee house I found. You can meet some interesting people at those places, and I always enjoy my experiences. The shop I ended up at yesterday is a gem."

"That sounds good." She smiled, finished her juice, and took one more sip of coffee as the server returned with Christopher's breakfast.

"Perfect timing," she added. "I'm going to get going, and hopefully we'll meet up at the pool after lunch to chat a little more. I'm thinking we may have quite a few other things in common." She winked as she stood.

Christopher stood also and smiled. "I think you might be right. Well, either way, enjoy your hike. Hopefully I'll see you a little later."

With that, Madeline pushed her chair back into place, then turned and walked out of the restaurant.

Christopher sat back down, now with a feeling he hadn't experienced in quite a while . . . could it have been a little dose of happiness? True to form, however, he wondered when the other shoe was going to fall. It wasn't like him to be negative, but as Lou McGraw had noticed yesterday, Christopher seemed to wear "the look of unluckiness." Fortunately, it wasn't apparent to Madeline. Somehow, he felt like the unluckiness had drifted away as they talked for a few minutes. If only he could make that feeling permanent . . .

Christopher finished his scrumptious breakfast, then stood and stared out the restaurant window again at the majestic mountains. A fog encircled the peaks, but the scene was getting brighter, and he stood transfixed by the increasingly sunny view. *Maybe it's a sign that things are going to start looking up for the world's unluckiest man. That would truly be a miracle.*

He tore his gaze away and walked briskly back to the room to brush his teeth. Once done, he grabbed a book to take with him to the coffee shop. There had been some kind of energy in the place that he just felt good about, and he wanted to get back there. He slipped on his flip flops, grabbed the keys, and jumped in his car instead of walking to the shop today.

As he pulled out of the driveway, he saw Madeline walking toward the hiking trails. He gave her a quick wave and drove on.

Once he reached the shop, he saw it was buzzing with activity. It almost seemed like a different place, were it not for Sam behind the counter. As Christopher approached, the young man immediately recognized him.

"Hey, welcome back!" The barista's smile brought some comfort to the out-of-towner and gave him the confidence to make small talk.

"Sam, how long have you worked here?"

The barista stroked his chin in thought. "I think it's three and a half years this week. I've been working my way through Covenant College, and I graduate in December," he said proudly.

"Wow, that's impressive! Where's home?"

"I call Lookout Mountain home now. I grew up in southeast Louisiana, but I guess you could say I didn't have the greatest childhood. As soon as I could get away, I did. Been here ever since—and I love it."

Christopher shrugged. "I guess we're all on our own journey, huh?"

The young man nodded and grinned. "Yes, and running into Lou was the best thing that's happened to me on my journey."

Christopher tilted his head. "Lucky Lou?"

"Absolutely. When I first got to town, I came to the coffee shop. Lou walked up and started talking to me—

just like he did with you yesterday—and I immediately felt like I had a friend."

Christopher nodded. "Funny, that's the way I felt, too. It's like he knows when people need to be seen and heard, huh?"

"Right. In fact, he's over there." The barista nodded toward a small table in the front. "He said if you happened to come in, to put your coffee on his tab and send you over to his table."

Christopher wore a look of surprise. "Really? How did he . . ."

The barista broke in and laughed. "Don't even try to guess. I mean, he's . . . Lucky. Who knows?" Sam handed Christopher a cup of coffee. "When I saw you come in, I poured your drink, so here you are."

The New Mexico man couldn't help but shake his head and smile. He thanked Sam and headed over to where Lucky was sitting, with Lep at his feet.

When Christopher approached, Lucky rose and gestured toward the seat across from him. "I had a feeling I might see you today." His eyes crinkled.

Christopher raised a brow and pulled the chair back, then sat down slowly. "I'm not sure how you knew I'd be coming back this morning, but it's good to see you, Lucky Lou." He smiled, then looked down, adding, "Good to see you too, Lep."

Lucky's furry friend wagged his tail vigorously and then leaned in to let Christopher stroke his head.

"How was your night at the inn?"

"Better than I expected. I mean, I didn't know what it would be like since it was the first time back there without my wife."

Lou acted unsurprised by this information, adding, "Yes, I can imagine that was different. Did you make any new friends?" He smiled.

Christopher cocked his head. "Yes, I—wait, how do you know about that?"

Lou grinned. "I really didn't. But even though I said you seemed a little unlucky, I sensed you had it in you. I had a feeling you're a people magnet."

Christopher set his coffee down. "Well, I used to be. But now, I'm a magnet for anything *but* goodness. In fact, I'm really surprised the woman I met wanted to talk to me this morning. She seems really . . . *nice*."

"Ah, she clearly has an instinct for kindhearted people. Who is this person?"

"Her name is Madeline. I might meet up with her later this afternoon. Unfortunately, she's headed out of town, so I won't likely see her again after that."

Lou shrugged and said evenly, "Never know." He sipped on his coffee.

Christopher took this as an opportunity to change the subject. "Lou, let me ask you something . . ."

"Ask away."

"People say you're the luckiest guy around. Are you *really* lucky?"

He stroked his neatly trimmed beard. "You know, I get asked that a lot. Let me ask *you* a question first: What do you consider 'luck'?"

Christopher turned his eyes to the ceiling, searching for the right words. He dropped his gaze down to his coffee, took a sip, and replied, "You know, it's when everything goes your way."

"Ah, yes, in that case . . . I'm *definitely* lucky."

The younger man shook his head and leaned away, crossing his arms. "See, that's not my life at all. Very little goes my way these days—and that's the truth."

Lucky cocked his head. "The truth, huh? Well, what do you mean by *your* way?"

"Like I want it to go, of course."

Lucky raised an eyebrow. "So, if things don't go the way *you* think they should go, you're not lucky?"

"Um, I guess."

Lucky raked his fingers through his thick hair. "The difference with me is, I was blessed long ago with the realization that life is short. I decided I'm okay with whatever happens to me, so in my opinion, everything *is* going my way. Therefore, by your definition, yes, I'm lucky. Hey, you alright?"

Christopher felt a bead of sweat roll down his face. He stared off into the distance. "I'm . . . not sure. I'm feeling a little, I don't know, dizzy maybe."

"Well, here, have some water."

Lucky handed him a glass. As Christopher started to sip the cool water, he fell to the floor and landed beside Lep, who let out a bark. Lucky flung his chair back, then reached down and felt the pulse on Christopher's neck.

He turned to Sam across the room and yelled as he began administering chest compressions, "I think he's having a heart attack—call 911!"

# Chapter Four

Most of the people in the shop had cleared out when the ambulance arrived a few minutes later, and as the two paramedics rushed in, the remaining customers quickly moved out of the way. Next to Christopher, who was still conscious, knelt Lucky and Sam. Lep lay quietly off to the side of his clearly concerned master.

One of the first responders started an EKG and checked Christopher's pulse. He made a noncommittal noise at the readings before saying, "Performing CPR may have saved his life, Lucky."

With that, the two paramedics put Christopher on a stretcher and lifted the drowsy victim into the back of the ambulance waiting just outside the shop entrance.

"I'd like to follow you gentlemen to the hospital if that's okay," Lucky offered.

"Of course. Does he have any relatives we can call?"

Before Lucky could answer, Christopher struggled to sit up and speak. The paramedic pushed him gently back down and Christopher rasped, "No! My family won't care at this point—*please* don't call them!"

He closed his eyes and winced as the two emergency workers exchanged bewildered glances. They turned to Lou who was standing outside the ambulance.

He shrugged. "I'll meet you there."

They nodded and closed the doors. Sirens blaring, the ambulance then made a hasty exit toward the hospital four miles away. Once at the emergency room, the staff jumped out and lowered Christopher out of the ambulance. They rushed him inside and down the hall, then the double doors swung shut so the doctors and staff could get to work.

Lucky arrived just seconds afterward, and as he entered the waiting area, he was greeted by the two paramedics.

"How is he?" Lucky blurted out.

"Stable, for now," one of them said. "On the way here, we administered aspirin and nitroglycerin, plus had him on oxygen, so his vitals are good. As I said, your quick action was key in helping him stay with us. The doctors are doing everything they can now."

His partner pressed Lucky. "Don't know who his relatives are?"

"No. We've just gotten to know each other. He's visiting from New Mexico, and as you heard, he and his family aren't close right now. I believe him when he says he doesn't want any of them contacted."

The men shook their heads in unison. Lucky thanked them, then walked over to one of the cloth-backed metal chairs to wait for the official prognosis. But before he could sit down, a nurse approached him.

"The doctor has confirmed Mr. Stone had a heart attack. You were with him when it happened, right?"

Lucky nodded solemnly.

"I understand he doesn't want his family contacted. We've gotten his medical information from his wallet, so we pretty much have what we need from an insurance perspective, but . . . would you consider being our point of contact until other arrangements can be made? We asked Mr. Stone, and he was able to give consent—that is, if it's alright with you."

Lucky Lou did not hesitate. "Gladly."

The nurse handed over a short form for his approval, and Lucky scribbled his signature on it.

"Thank you. They're putting in a stent now, and we'll keep you posted as things progress. Hopefully we'll have good news. . . ."

Lou smiled in thanks at the nurse, who then pivoted and walked back down the hall to her station.

After lunch, a middle-aged man in surgical scrubs approached. "Mr. McGraw?"

Lucky stood. "Yes."

"Your friend is going to make it. We've successfully inserted a stent. It could have been much, much worse—although any coronary event is nothing to trivialize."

Lucky let out a breath. "Can I see him?"

"Let's wait a few hours. The anesthesia will have worn off by then, and he should be able to talk to you. They tell me he doesn't want relatives notified, correct?" The doctor raised a curious eyebrow.

Lucky shrugged his shoulders. "I know it's unusual, and it seems counterintuitive in a situation like this, but . . . it's his choice, and that's what he said he wants—or rather, *doesn't* want."

The doctor shook his head. "If you say so. Just have a seat, Mr. McGraw, and we'll let you know when he's ready for visitors."

Lucky placed his hand appreciatively on the man's shoulder. "Thank you."

The doctor smiled in return, then pivoted and walked away, disappearing behind the heavy metal doors.

Lucky sat back down, looked toward the ceiling, and exhaled once more. The day had certainly not gone in the direction he had expected. *What next?* he thought. *What will happen to Christopher? How will he handle the weeks of recovery ahead?* Lou slumped in the chair, rubbing his temples as he waited for the next update.

Three hours later, a young nurse entered the waiting room and approached Lou. "The doctor said you can visit Mr. Stone now." She smiled reassuringly. "I'm sure he'll be glad to see you. Right this way . . ."

Lou followed her through the open doors and down a wide hallway until they reached a room with the door slightly ajar.

The nurse knocked and called out, "Mr. Stone, there's someone to see you—it's Mr. McGraw."

Christopher's voice sounded surprisingly steady as he replied, "Please let him in, and thank you, Nurse."

She nudged the door open and offered a sweeping gesture as Lucky entered the room, then she softly pulled the door closed behind him.

Lucky began, "Well, if you wanted to bring some excitement to our coffee talks, this was one way to do it—though I'm not sure I would recommend an encore." His eyes twinkled.

"Ha, yeah, I figured it would get me a free cup of coffee—oh, wait, you had already put it on your tab. What a waste of drama," Christopher offered back with a weak chuckle.

Lucky smiled, but his tone was more sober now. "How are you feeling?"

"Like I got run over by a train."

"I can only imagine."

Christopher continued, "I really had no idea how bad my stress was. I mean, I knew I'd been under a lot of pressure, and my life has been anxiety-ridden for years, but I didn't know I was at *this* point." He turned away from Lou in embarrassment.

"Sometimes we don't know we're close to a breaking point until we actually break," Lucky said gently.

"Yeah, but now . . . I lost my chance to have one last conversation with Madeline before she took off. Unlucky again . . ." He rolled his eyes.

At that moment, there came a knock on the door.

"Come in," Christopher called out dejectedly.

The nurse entered with a large, decorative vase full of colorful flowers.

"What? Who are those for? Surely not *me*." He looked over at Lucky in astonishment.

"They most certainly are," the nurse responded brightly as she set the flowers on a dresser near the bed before leaving once again.

"Lucky, would you read the card for me?" Christopher pointed to a small envelope nestled snugly in the arrangement.

Lucky nodded and removed the note from its sleeve. He read aloud:

*Dear Christopher,*

*I was so sad to hear what happened! When I didn't see you at the pool, I assumed you didn't want to meet after all—or that something had come up—so I went ahead and got on the road. Shortly after that, I got the news!*

*I trust you are recovering—I have an acquaintance at the hospital who tells me you are already doing better.*

*I am sorry we won't have the chance to spend more time together. I'm already outside of Atlanta on my travels, and I think I'll continue on to Florida.*

*Then again, maybe we'll be lucky, and our paths will cross again. I truly hope so . . .*

*Madeline*

Christopher closed his eyes, shrinking further into the hospital bed. "How ironic—she mentioned she hoped we would be 'lucky' that our paths would cross. Clearly, she didn't know who she was dealing with. It's probably for the best—for *her* anyway."

Lucky turned his gaze to the window overlooking the hospital courtyard for a moment. "Do you remember when I told you I've learned to be okay with everything in my life?"

Christopher nodded.

"Well, I didn't say it wasn't painful sometimes, because it is. But, I do believe there is a bigger plan at work, even when I don't understand it. It might be time for you to start seeing your life in the same way."

He hesitated, and then added with a reassuring wink, "That is, if you want to take the first step for getting in the lucky club."

Christopher managed a slight smile. "Thanks, Lou. I suppose I have lots of lessons coming my way. Already this whole ordeal has been a wake-up call for me."

The two talked for a few more minutes until Lucky saw the patient's eyelids grow heavy. "You rest now. I'll be back later, and we can talk more. I need to go home and check on Lep—one of the coffee shop employees was kind enough to bring him to my place when everything started happening."

Christopher nodded wearily and pulled the covers up to his chin as Lucky stepped quietly out of the room.

# CHAPTER FIVE

The next morning, Lucky drove to the hospital to check on Christopher's progress. When he arrived, the receptionist greeted him by name before pointing the visitor back to his friend's room.

Lou knocked once, then tentatively pushed the door open just as Christopher turned toward him.

"Lucky! Great to see you."

"How are you feeling today, Christopher?"

"Better, thanks."

Lucky smiled and placed a small suitcase on the floor near him. "I stopped by the Magnolia and picked up some of your clothes and toiletry items. The innkeeper is a friend of mine, and she heard about what happened, so she let me into your room—hope that's okay."

"Of course, thank you. But I started thinking this morning . . ." His voice trailed off.

Lucky tilted his head. "Yes?"

"The doctor said I should be able to go home on Monday, after I see the cardio rehab staff. I don't know what I'm going to do since I don't have a 'home' nearby. I sure don't want to go back to Albuquerque in a couple of days. . . ."

Lucky nodded. "I've actually been thinking about that, too."

Christopher's brows drew together in anticipation.

"You should come live with me for a while."

Christopher shook his head. "No, no, I couldn't impose. Thank you, Lucky, but—"

Lucky held up a hand to stop him. "No question— that's what we're going to do." He grinned. "Do you have a person you trust with the business while you're gone?"

Christopher nodded.

"Good, so that's taken care of. You're going to need some assistance getting back on track, and I have a wonderful housekeeper who lives with me. She'll be happy to help."

"But—"

Lou held up his hand again. "Oh yeah, one more thing. We're going to get you into the lucky club."

Doubt dawned on Christopher's face, but Lucky continued, unfazed. "To do that, there are some things you'll need to learn—five things, as a matter of fact."

"Five?" Christopher echoed.

"Yes, and if you're finally ready to get back to feeling that life is working *for* you instead of against you, I'll teach you these five lucky secrets. What do you think?"

Christopher nodded adamantly. "You're on!"

"Excellent! I was thinking your recovery time would be the perfect opportunity for me to teach you. Besides, we'll need to take some field trips for these lessons, and I'm one of the few people who know where to go."

Christopher's puzzled expression didn't go unnoticed by Lucky Lou. "Listen, you're going to have to trust me. It doesn't take a genius to see that you've hit rock bottom with this heart attack."

Christopher looked sheepish but was listening intently now.

"It also doesn't take a genius to see that you're a good person with a good heart. I can teach people the skills of a 'lucky' life, but I can't teach a person to have a kind spirit like yours, so you're a terrific candidate. This is the perfect chance for you to make a fresh start. Who knows, maybe this will be the beginning of a life you could never have dreamed of—and the 'unlucky' things may have been exactly what were needed to lead you toward this new and much better life."

The shocked expression on Christopher's face gave way to excitement. "Lucky, if you would do that, I don't know how I could ever repay you."

Lucky's gaze lingered toward the window before turning back to his new friend. "First, I have a sense you and I have some significant things in common. Second, this would be a win-win."

Christopher tilted his head. "W-what do you mean?"

Lucky spoke haltingly as his eyes bore into Christopher's. "Let's just say a debt has been weighing on me, and it's time to pay it back. . . ."

As the doctor had hoped, Christopher was scheduled for discharge on Monday. Having the weekend in the hospital turned out to be a mixed bag—while it gave him the time he needed to rest and recover, under a doctor's supervision, it also gave him long stretches to think about what had gotten him to the point of this mental and physical meltdown.

Monday morning, lying in the silence of his room, he thought back on the rumors going all over town that he and Sarah were getting divorced, before he had even realized she wanted out of their marriage. In hindsight, it was clear she was unhappy: the diminishing conversations, her lack of interest in his work, the desire to go out with her friends as opposed to spending time with him—

*Knock knock.*

"Lucky!"

Christopher pushed himself up to sit straighter in the bed as Lucky stepped in, followed by the doctor who had now been assigned to Christopher's case.

The physician nodded at Lucky, who cheerfully announced, "This fine gentleman says you are ready to depart the building!"

"That is, unless you'd like to stay with us a little longer," the doctor chimed in with a grin.

"No offense, Doc, but I think I've worn out my welcome here—or at least, that's my story, and I'm sticking to it."

All three men laughed, and then the physician stepped toward his patient and handed him a clipboard with some paperwork to complete. "Just a few places to sign, and you'll be on your way."

Lucky smiled broadly. "Thanks for all you folks have done. I promise I'll take good care of the old boy."

"Good to hear," said the doctor. "Your friend is doing exceptionally well and should be ready to ramp up his exercise. I'd just like to see him back in a week to make sure he's continuing to heal."

Christopher spoke up, beaming. "I'll make sure not to run any marathons between now and then."

Handing the completed forms back to the doctor, he then turned to Lucky. "Give me a few minutes to get all this stuff together, and I'll be ready. First, we need to stop by the inn so I can officially check out."

Lucky shook his head. "Already done. I got all your remaining things taken over to my house, and I settled up with the innkeeper. She's letting you leave your car there for as long as you'd like."

Christopher reached out to shake Lucky's hand. "You're a true friend, Lou. I can see why you're so popular around here—in addition to your good luck, of course." He winked.

Lucky smiled. "I'll wait in the hallway while you pack up. Your chariot—er, I mean, wheelchair—is waiting for your mandatory ride out the front door. We'll have you to my place in no time at all."

Feeling a great deal more cheerful, Christopher began gathering his few belongings and in less than ten minutes, he was calling for his friend. "Ready when you are, Lucky Lou!"

With assistance from a nurse, Lucky guided his pal into the wheelchair, and the trio took the elevator down to the first floor where Lucky's vehicle—a red 1967 pickup truck—awaited. The staff waved a collective goodbye, and Christopher smiled broadly as the pair began their journey.

The drive through Lookout Mountain to get to Lou's was short but filled with breathtaking vistas and exquisite stone houses. Along the way, there were occasional opportunities to look out over the mountains and admire the picturesque views of Chattanooga below.

"How long have you lived here, Lucky?"

"Let me think . . . twenty-two years."

"And before that?"

"I lived in New York for a short time, then New England for many years." Lucky added, "But I grew up in a little place called Belfast."

"As in . . . Belfast, *Ireland?*"

He pointed playfully. "That's the one—specifically, Northern Ireland. You wouldn't expect a lucky man to be from anywhere else, would you?"

"Now that I think about it, no, it doesn't surprise me. I want to visit there someday—it's on my bucket list."

"Well, maybe you'll get there sooner than you think." Lou's eyes sparkled.

Christopher raised an eyebrow at the curious comment. "If you say so."

Lou pointed to a modest dwelling just up ahead. "We'll turn right on the street after that house—Mr. McWilliam's home—and then it's only about another mile down the road."

"Sounds good," Christopher replied. "Do you know most of your neighbors by name?"

Lucky said matter-of-factly, "I make it a point to know all of them—that is, all of them who *want* to be known."

Christopher nodded. "Most folks in my neighborhood back in Albuquerque like to keep to themselves—not that there's anything wrong with that."

Lou steered the truck onto the street after the McWilliam house. "When I grew up in Belfast, it would have been unheard of not to know your neighbors. But then again, during that time you leaned on each other a lot because there was so much conflict in the country. You know, the whole Protestant versus Catholic thing."

"That makes sense. I know there were lots of problems for a long time in Northern Ireland. That period of conflict was called . . . let me think . . . The Troubles?"

"You know your Irish history," said Lucky, impressed. "Yes, The Troubles were a time when we all wondered if the country was going to be torn apart or brought together. In the end, I'd say it was a little of both."

Christopher nodded. "I remember studying that in school. It began in the late sixties and lasted about thirty years, right?"

Lou rubbed his chin. "Yes, you're not far off. It lasted until nineteen ninety-eight, and over 3,500 people died." He shook his head. "The Protestant Unionists wanted to remain part of the United Kingdom. The

Catholic nationalists, on the other hand, wanted unification with the Republic of Ireland."

Lou waved his hand as if to change the subject. "Anyway, enough about Irish politics for now—we've made it. Home sweet home!" He pointed in the distance to a splendid three-story brown and beige stone house at the end of a winding drive.

Christopher's jaw dropped. "Lucky, that is . . . *quite* a place—it's like a castle!"

Lou smiled and turned onto the asphalt driveway, cruising past vast acres of green pasture. A few sheep grazed on one side, and a small gaggle of geese waddled by a large, oval-shaped pond on the other side. The entire length of the driveway was lined with freshly painted white picket fence.

"It looks like Ireland!" Christopher couldn't contain his excitement as he spoke. "At least, what I imagine Ireland looks like—the thick, green grass, the sheep, the stone house, and the gently curving driveway."

Lucky nodded. "Exactly! I designed it to remind me of my homeland every time I drive up."

As the two got closer to the house, Christopher grew quiet, taking in the scene. The flowers, the trees, the lawn, all had a distinct Irish feel—or what he assumed it would "feel" like there.

When they pulled up to the entrance of the home, an attractive, middle-aged woman stepped out to greet them. She was wearing a black-and-grey housekeeper's uniform, and she had long, silky red hair which was pulled back into a ponytail, framing the flawless, pale white skin of her face.

She walked up to the passenger side of the truck and opened the door for Christopher with a smile. "Gentlemen, welcome!"

Lucky stepped out and greeted her. "Maggie O'Doulle, this is my friend Christopher." He gestured toward his passenger.

At that moment, Lep appeared, wagging his tail excitedly. Maggie turned to the dog and said playfully, "I know, it's your new friend, but you'll have to wait." Lucky called for Lep, who obediently trotted over to his side, so Maggie could help their guest out of the car.

Christopher stuck out his hand in greeting. "Hi, Maggie, I'm Christopher Stone. It's nice to meet you. I'm grateful you've both allowed me to come and recover here."

She smiled and shook his outstretched hand. "Aw, it's a pleasure, Mr. Stone. Let me get your luggage."

Lucky gently waved her away as Lep began to yelp. "I'll take care of the luggage—and Lep. Could you just walk my friend inside, please?"

Maggie held onto Christopher's right arm and led him into the house through the pristine double-paned front door. As they stepped in, Christopher's gaze rose to the vaulted ceiling and the strikingly large chandelier that hovered above the spacious, sunken den. The walls were constructed with spectacular stone.

"It's magnificent, Maggie. What a beautiful home."

The attendant nodded. "Yes, it's a beauty. Mr. McGraw designed it himself."

"Even more impressive," Christopher added. "How long have you been with him?"

The woman smiled broadly. "Ten years. My family came from Ireland to America when I was quite young. Many years later, I answered an ad for a full-time housekeeper, and I got hired. I've been with Mr. McGraw ever since, and I feel really *lucky* to have ended up here." She winked.

Maggie then waved her hand in a sweeping gesture. "You're welcome anywhere in the house, but your room will be on the ground floor to make it easier for you while you're healing. I can take you there now, if you'll just follow me."

Christopher walked behind her, slowly but without assistance, enjoying the smallest bit of independence. Once across the den, Maggie turned down a narrow hallway, then stepped into the first room.

She looked back to Christopher and cheerfully announced, "Here you are, sir!"

Christopher crossed the threshold and took in the vastness of the space, decorated in a tasteful Irish theme. The walls were papered with whimsical, colorful scenes such as narrow trails through shadowy woods leading to quaint thatched cottages, and plenty of cheerful interactions over drinks in neighborhood pubs.

"I just love this!"

Maggie beamed. "Excellent, sir. I trust if there's anything you need during your stay, you'll let me know." With that, she reached to close the door behind her and quietly left the room.

As Christopher sat down on the edge of the Victorian four-poster bed, he let out a breath of relief. There was a comforting aura here—not only in his room, but in the entire home. He couldn't put his finger on it, but as odd as it seemed, he almost had the feeling of becoming . . . *luckier*. He chided himself internally. It was nonsensical to think he could borrow luck from a house, however grandiose it was.

Just then, Lucky trudged in, laden with the two red suitcases. "I believe these are yours, my good man." He set the suitcases down at the far end of the room.

Christopher smiled. "Lucky, I'm so thankful to be here. I feel like I'm healing already, as crazy as that sounds."

Lucky cocked his head, and a sly smile spread across his face. "It might not be as crazy as you think. Just enjoy your time here, and let's get you feeling better."

Christopher nodded in appreciation.

"We'll have dinner at seven, and I think you'll find Maggie is a tremendous cook. Afterwards, I'll share a few things about my homeland and, if you're open to it, some ideas that you might find enlightening." His eyes sparkled.

"Lucky, I am open to anything you have to say to me. Not only am I grateful for your hospitality, but I am also glad that you're willing to help get my mental health back. I've been a total wreck, and meeting you at the coffee shop was the first time I felt like someone cared about me getting better. Thanks to you, I'm slowly starting to climb out of a very dark place. I don't know how I was fortunate enough to meet you."

Lucky nodded. "I believe we were meant to find each other. In fact, I would say it was 'good luck' for both of us." The corners of his mouth turned up.

Lucky Lou walked to the door and then turned back to Christopher. "See you at seven o'clock, my friend."

He shut the door softly, and Christopher noted the time on his watch: *5:59.*

Immediately, a chill ran through him as he recalled the significance of that exact moment two years ago. . . .

# Chapter Six

The dinner was a spectacular Gaelic meal—homemade stew, buttered egg noodles, and roasted vegetables from the farmers' market in nearby Rising Fawn. To finish, Maggie brought each of the men a cup of coffee and shots of Irish whiskey, which they blended, then sipped slowly.

Christopher was first to break the comfortable silence. "Lucky, let me ask you . . . do you think our meeting in the coffee shop was just a coincidence? In the hospital, you said something about how meeting me benefited you. Is that true?"

Lucky took a long sip of his coffee and then stood. "Let's go get comfortable in the den, Christopher. I think you are going to be interested in what I have to say."

The two moved into the large den, and Maggie followed with fresh coffee. She set the cups on the small cherry tables next to the burgundy Queen Ann chairs that were arranged across from each other.

Lucky began, "I've told very few people what I'm about to share with you."

Christopher leaned in.

"I lived in Northern Ireland during The Troubles, the period you mentioned earlier. As I said, it was a violent era for our country, but it was also a painful time for my family. One fall afternoon in Belfast, I was outside playing stickball with my father and my best friend, Sean, in our normally peaceful neighborhood. I was seventeen. It was a Sunday, the sky was blue, the air was crisp, and everything seemed perfect. . . ."

Christopher crinkled his brow as Lucky paused, trying to gather his composure.

"There were two loud crashing sounds, as if glass was hitting concrete. Someone had thrown a couple of Molotov cocktails—crude explosive devices—in our direction, and they hit right between my dad and Sean. My father was killed almost instantly."

Lucky's story tumbled out with increasing speed as though he were trying to forget it ever happened. "Sean was burning so badly, and I needed something to put out the flames. I ran inside the house and grabbed a blanket. As I rolled him in it, he was screaming in pain. I just can't get that image out of my mind, even today."

Lucky put his head in his hands.

"I'm so sorry, Lucky. I—I had no idea. . . ."

Lucky shook his head, took a deep breath, and wiped tears from his eyes. "Mother came running out at the commotion. When she saw my father's lifeless, charred body, she ran over and tried to pick him up, but he was in such awful shape. Minutes later, an ambulance arrived with two men who jumped out to assist Sean, still in agony. They took him to a burn unit at a hospital about twenty minutes away, but soon afterwards, he died."

Christopher couldn't believe what he was hearing. "This is just horrible."

Lucky hung his head. "It was a day I'll never forget. Shortly after, my mother and I moved to a small town just east of Belfast, where we lived until I was twenty-one. That year, she passed away, and I decided to leave the country since I felt there was no reason to stay."

Christopher said grimly, "That's a heavy cross to bear."

Lucky slowly lifted his eyes toward his friend. "Yes, but here is something important to remember, Christopher: broken people can become some of the luckiest of all."

Christopher's forehead wrinkled in confusion.

"It's true. People who, like me, have dealt with tragedy often develop an acute understanding that life is short. Once you know this, you count your blessings, and you're much more likely to allow life to unfold rather than try and stop it or force things to go your way. I feel *lucky* that I learned this early on in my life."

Lucky leaned forward, and his eyes narrowed. "But there's much more to this story. . . . When my mother passed, I inherited something that turned out to be unique, sacred—and extremely powerful."

He stood and motioned for his friend to follow him down the hallway to a door Christopher hadn't noticed earlier. Opening the door, Lucky revealed a spiral wrought iron staircase. Lep, who had been roused from his nap by their movement, was now excitedly tagging along. They proceeded cautiously down it into a beautifully designed finished basement.

"Have a seat over there, Christopher." He pointed to a beige wooden chair beside a small matching table.

Christopher looked curiously toward Lucky, who had turned away to remove a large, framed map of Ireland, which had covered a wall safe. His fingers began nimbly manipulating the dial, and when the tumblers clicked, the door popped open, and Lucky reached in. He withdrew what appeared to be an ancient, chestnut-colored scroll.

Christopher's eyes grew wide. "W-what is *that?*" he stuttered.

Slowly, Lucky pulled the relic open about six inches, revealing an expanding sheet of parchment paper with what appeared to be Gaelic lettering. He set the opened scroll in Christopher's lap.

Christopher lifted it gently and then squinted at the wording. "Of course, I have *no* idea what it says."

Lucky laughed and said, "I assumed your fifth-century Gaelic was a little rusty."

He sat down in a wooden chair beside his friend, and Christopher carefully placed the relic on the table between them.

"Christopher, have you heard of St. Patrick?"

"I may be from Albuquerque, but yes, I know of St. Patrick—he lived in the mid four hundreds."

Lucky grinned in approval. "Go on. What else?"

Christopher continued, now tapping his chin. "Well, St. Patrick's Day is named after him, of course. He's supposedly the guy who drove the snakes out of Ireland, and there are legends about him teaching with shamrocks . . . or something like that."

Lucky nodded. "Whether those legends about snakes and shamrocks are true, I don't know. But I do know St. Patrick is *not* made up."

Lucky glanced pointedly at the parchment, and Christopher's mouth fell open at what his new mentor said next:

"His words on this scroll have guided my life for many years."

"But . . . how did you get it?" Christopher breathed.

Lucky shook his head. "That's where it gets odd. My mother and I had moved outside of Belfast, and one rainy fall night, an older gentleman in a black suit and a black derby hat knocked on our door. The man handed her a bejeweled metal container. He then tipped his hat, bowed, and said quietly, 'The luck of Saint Patrick . . . is rightfully yours.'"

"My mother was in such shock, she didn't know how to respond. She pried open the container and saw the scroll inside, then when she looked back up, the man had faded into the night. She called after him, but he was gone, never to be seen again. Still today, I don't know who it was."

Christopher gasped. "Are you serious?"

Lucky calmly continued. "Of course, my mother didn't know anything about Gaelic either, and she assumed it was all just a prank—she was a cynical person anyway, and when my dad died, she became even more so. In fact, I think the whole bizarre affair frightened her. And yet, she didn't get rid of the scroll. She temporarily stuffed it in the back of her bedroom closet, but unfortunately passed away a year later, never having known the power of the relic."

Christopher sat in awe. "I'm guessing the fact that everyone thinks you are the luckiest person around has something to do with this scroll from the fifth century."

Lucky arched his eyebrows. "It has *everything* to do with that."

Christopher scratched his head. "So . . . you inherited the scroll. But how did you find out about the authenticity of it—and are you going to tell me what it says, or *what?*" He smiled.

"Not so fast!" Lucky said. "There's a lot here, even if it looks like it's just a simple scroll."

Christopher leaned back, held up his hands, and chuckled. "Okay, okay, I gotcha."

"The road was long to determining the authenticity of the scroll. I decided to get out of Ireland when my mother passed—as I said, there was nothing left for me there. When I was packing everything, I found the container with its perplexing content. I shoved it into a moving box, thinking I would deal with it some other time. 'Some other time' ended up being much, much later—after my divorce, sadly . . ." His voice trailed off.

"I'm sorry. I didn't know."

Lucky was clearly not interested in elaborating. "Anyway, I had made it to America. I took the container and the scroll to a university in Connecticut where an expert linguist and archeologist confirmed the scroll originated in the fifth century A.D. He also verified the author was . . . Saint Patrick."

Christopher exhaled loudly and palmed his neck. He opened his mouth to speak, but before he could, Lucky added, "The document is titled 'THE FIVE SECRETS OF LUCK.'"

"Now, *that's* exactly what I need!" Christopher exclaimed, rubbing his hands together.

Lucky merely smiled and continued, "It turns out St. Patrick had an unthinkably difficult life as a youth—especially for someone known for being lucky. There's a lot we don't know about him, but we *do* know he was kidnapped by Irish pirates at age sixteen while living with his successful, high-profile family in Britain."

Christopher's pupils grew large as Lucky kept going.

"He was taken to Ireland and forced to work as a sheep herder, but he made an incredible escape six years later and returned home. Patrick felt so blessed to have survived and to have reconnected with his old life that he came to believe it was divine intervention. From that point on, he began experiencing more and more blessings, against all odds, which he couldn't otherwise explain."

Christopher folded his arms, shaking his head slowly. "Fascinating . . ."

Lucky nodded, then leaned in closer. "Here's where it gets even *more* fascinating. Soon after he got back to Britain—and years before he entered the ministry—Patrick began traveling all over Europe, searching for 'lucky' outliers. He wanted to find people who, like himself, had encountered and conquered extraordinary challenges—people with 'charmed' lives. He was determined to learn what these individuals had in common."

Christopher sat on the edge of his seat as Lucky continued, "After finding and interviewing over a hundred of these 'lucky' people, he returned home having identified five highly spiritual common denominators."

Christopher's voice was quiet, but his excitement was palpable. "The Five Secrets of Luck."

"Exactly. Patrick maintained that living according to this unique combination of tenets—based on service, compassion, and courage—would make you, in a word, 'lucky'."

Christopher went slack-jawed. "So, *real* 'luck' is a lot more than just *chance*. . . ."

"Right, and that's critically important. Patrick's definition of 'lucky'—and yes, he coined the word in the fifth century—was 'a seemingly charmed state of existence which results from living in adherence to five spiritual enigmas.'"

Christopher massaged his temples. "Good grief, my head is spinning, Lucky."

Ignoring the comment, the Irishman pressed on. "And of course, luck is real because it is rooted in . . . faith."

"Yes, the power of faith," Christopher murmured, openmouthed.

"St. Patrick's discovery of these five spiritual secrets—and the resulting power of their combination—was nothing short of revolutionary."

Lucky paused to let that sink in, then said, "Unfortunately, in the Middle Ages, around the fourteenth or fifteenth century, his ideas had become morphed. People began ascribing a *much* different meaning to 'luck' than what St. Patrick originally wrote."

Christopher managed to stutter, "How, how so?"

"They began omitting the crucial part about *living in adherence to five spiritual enigmas*, and instead only focused on 'a seemingly charmed state of existence.' This radically diluted the definition of luck, defining it as a life of *random* good fortune. Unfortunately, that's still how most people think of it."

Christopher laced his fingers behind his head. "So, are there different levels of 'luck' that result from following the secrets in St. Patrick's *original* definition?"

"Yes," said Lucky in earnest. "The more closely one adheres to these principles, the more power they provide. Incidentally, there are still plenty of folks who get randomly 'lucky,' yet those who rigorously apply what St. Patrick taught—well, they're on another level."

"How many people know about the scroll and the secrets?"

Lucky's mouth twisted. "It's hard to say. After years of sharing the message in Britain, Patrick eventually returned to Ireland, and I'm sure he spread the message there, too. But, from what I've found in my research, the scroll disappeared right after he died in 461 A.D.—"

"—only to literally show up on your mom's doorstep fifteen hundred years later," Christopher said in awe.

Lucky shrugged. "Yes, for whatever reason. But to return to your question, no one can measure how widespread the knowledge and power are from The Five Secrets. Most people don't believe—or simply don't know—the scroll even exists. But I suppose if you know someone whose life seems to be incredibly, consistently 'lucky,' then they live out the secrets—intentionally or unintentionally."

Lucky held up a finger. "However . . . even though the scroll's influential precepts can transform your life, those benefits can also slip away quickly if the principles aren't followed."

"I think that's exactly why so much has happened to me," Christopher mused. "The benefits have slipped away—far, far away. Probably because I have neglected the principles . . . whatever they are." He laughed nervously.

"It doesn't mean we'll never be tested," Lucky said, "especially if we fall away from the principles, as I said. But you're getting ahead of me. . . .

"If you're ready, let's start going through these 'lucky secrets.' They'll take time, but you're not in a hurry, right?" He flashed a toothy grin.

Christopher smiled back. "I'm in no hurry—and I'm ready."

Lucky nodded and took a deep breath. "In that case, let's begin. . . ."

# CHAPTER SEVEN

Speaking with confidence and conviction, Lucky started his explanation of The Five Secrets of Luck.

"By the way, Christopher, as we talk about these secrets, I want you to use St. Patrick's definition of luck. Look through his lens of faith, not that of people seeking prosperity and ease by taking the shortcut approach. Remember, luck isn't random when you apply the secrets.

"Number one is . . .

## "THE SECRET OF LUCKY WORDS."

Christopher immediately felt sheepish. "Uh oh. I already have a feeling I'm going to get my toes stepped on."

Lucky Lou shook his head and laughed. "There's no judgment in any of this, buddy. Just do your best, and simply use the words of St. Patrick as a benchmark."

"A benchmark. I like that." Christopher stroked his chin.

Lucky continued. "All of the secrets contained in the scroll are important and interrelated, but using lucky words is the foundational principle. St. Patrick made it clear *nothing* else works if this concept is not in place."

Christopher leaned in.

"Now," Lucky went on, "it's so tempting to make comments like, 'Well, that's just my luck.' or, 'Yep, that's just like me, doing something stupid like that.' This complaining, negative language becomes a self-fulfilling prophecy, and most people talk like that every day. It's also contagious and drives luck away more than anything else."

Christopher cut in: "I can remember many times I used those exact phrases." He shook his head.

Lou spread his palms. "Of course, we all have! But the point is, we want to be aware of it so we can start dropping those phrases from our vocabulary. The more we label ourselves as 'unlucky' and talk about our limitations, the more we *believe* those labels and limitations, and the people around us become convinced of our inabilities also.

"Think about it: it's like if someone constantly told you that you were a failure, that you couldn't succeed, that you weren't capable. If you hear someone repeat it enough, you *believe* it. It works the same way— maybe even more so—when *we* are the ones saying it about ourselves."

Christopher snapped his fingers as if he had an epiphany. "I know exactly what you mean. Conversely, the more we talk about *good* things, and focus on what we *can* do, the more *we* start believing we're capable—maybe even 'lucky.' Plus, I imagine other people start seeing us as more capable and luckier." He beamed.

"You're right!" Lou enthusiastically pointed a finger at his friend.

Christopher was shaking his head. "As much as I hate to admit it, I can already see how far I have strayed from this philosophy—not only with myself, but with my family and friends and staff."

"Great!" Lucky exclaimed.

"Great? But that's not—"

"I mean great that you *realize* it. You've already taken the first step toward change. Minding our words is one of the most powerful ways to improve our lives. The best part is, it's no more difficult to use lucky language than it is to use unlucky language. It's just a matter of habit."

Christopher sat in silence, taking in what he was hearing. After a moment of solitude, he said softly, "This is such an eye-opener. I think about the times I tried to motivate myself or others by speaking harshly or threatening negative consequences. There's nothing 'lucky' about that kind of talk, and now I see it clearly."

Lou nodded. "Then you're way ahead of most people. Now, here's another part you have to remember about this secret—and it's important. . . ."

Christopher leaned forward.

"Don't make a big deal out of your perceived problems or difficulties."

Christopher cocked his head. "What do you mean by that?"

"Just like it sounds," Lucky said matter-of-factly. "When things don't go your way, don't draw too much attention to yourself by talking about them."

"Give me an example, Lucky."

"When you tell people about your divorce, or about some of the other 'bad' things that have happened to you, be mindful of how often you're doing so. A little discussion with the right people is therapeutic; a lot of discussion with too many people can become *theatrical*. It draws attention and energy to you, but not the lucky kind you want."

Christopher crossed his arms, and his brow furrowed. "So, you're saying don't talk to people about my difficulties?"

Lucky shook his head. "Not at all. I'm saying don't *broadcast* your problems. If you talk to others too much about your hardships, you're proclaiming how unlucky you are—which is what you'll become in their eyes, and maybe objectively to boot."

Lucky went on, "Good things can't happen if we spend too much time focused on bad things. Instead, sit with the difficulty awhile, and then if you want or need to talk about it with someone, by all means, do."

Christopher nodded, hanging on every word.

"Plus—and this is *key*—remember, when something goes 'wrong,' we don't know for sure that it's not ultimately a *good* thing. It's tempting to label it immediately as 'bad,' but it could lead us to something else that's *good*."

Christopher's mind was processing everything Lucky was saying. "So, if I'm blurting out to anyone who'll listen about the terrible struggles I've encountered, then I'm setting myself up for those events to lead to unfavorable outcomes. I'm also portraying myself as a victim because I'm focusing on how *bad* things are going for me instead of allowing space for the good that might also result."

Lou raised his shoulders. "It's true, you're programming your mind with 'bad luck' language. St. Patrick could have done the same thing after getting captured by pirates. It took incredible courage, but I assure you *goodness* was the focus in his language— written and verbal—not how terrible his life was."

Christopher grinned. "This is powerful, Lucky. I can see how you embody the first secret because you believe life is inherently good, and your discourse is a direct expression of that belief."

Lucky leaned back and took a deep breath. "Well, that's nice to hear. There have been plenty of times when things weren't going my way, but you'll seldom hear me talk about them. I say 'seldom' because there *are* times I share my struggles with someone I trust. But, I've always thought through the problem first, and then I carefully choose my next steps—that's the difference."

"I get it," Christopher said with a nod.

Lucky raised a finger. "One more thing about lucky language. The tone, the gentleness, and the quality of our words are all important. If we're speaking harshly, anxiously, or carelessly, we're sharing and perpetuating our lack of confidence and faith. We're again unknowingly articulating how unlucky we are—and driving away good fortune and opportunity."

Christopher's excitement was evident as he shook his head. "I had never given any thought to how important my words are. This is so empowering!"

Lucky applauded him. "You're off to a great start, my friend, and I think you're going to love the next secret too. But it's getting late, so let me escort you back to your room for a good night's rest. Tomorrow we'll go for a ride through the mountains, and I'll tell you about The Second Secret of Luck."

Christopher realized his eyelids were indeed getting heavy as Lucky stood up, put the scroll back in the safe, and replaced the map on the wall. The two men then climbed the spiral staircase, with Lep close behind, and Lucky escorted Christopher to the guest room for the evening.

When they reached his door, Christopher extended his hand. "Thank you again, Lucky. I already feel like my life is taking a step forward—and I've often doubted that would be the case again."

Lucky smiled broadly and shook the man's outstretched hand. "There are good days ahead. Trust me."

Christopher smiled back and then turned, closing the door behind him. He sank onto the bed, exhaled loudly, and said under his breath, "I hope so, Lou. I really hope so. . . ."

# CHAPTER EIGHT

Christopher, despite feeling encouraged after his conversation with Lou on the first secret of luck, tossed and turned throughout the night. Thoughts plagued him of his wife, of Megan, of anything and everything that could—or had—gone wrong in his life.

He reflected on the times he should have used the "lucky language" Lou told him about—in particular, when Megan had come to him with her challenges as a teen. Instead of offering encouragement, he had tried to "fix" her problems for her, or he had simply lectured her on how she shouldn't have gotten into difficulty in the first place. He didn't realize how much his own stress was gradually affecting his language—and consequently, his relationships.

If only he had used words that were soothing, encouraging, empowering, and then allowed Megan to solve her own problems. She was more than capable. As he considered her journey to adulthood, it was clear she was extremely smart, even wise. . . .

Christopher put a pillow over his head and turned over, but the intrusive thoughts did not let up. Finally, the alarm sounded at eight o'clock, and he jumped out of bed—hoping to escape the mental anguish.

At that second, however, he felt a different sort of pain—a small, dull pain in his chest, and he realized he wasn't quite ready to get back to a "normal" life yet. The doctor had warned him to be patient—something Christopher wasn't very good at, even when he was well.

Just then, there was a knock at the door followed by Lucky's concerned voice. "Okay in there, friend? I heard the alarm go off and thought it might have been a mistake. . . ."

"Come on in, Lucky."

Lucky entered and plopped down in an old rocking chair beside the bed, while Christopher sank into a nearby wicker chair.

"Yeah, I've never been too good at sleeping in," Christopher admitted. "I want to get up and hit the ground running, every day. I know I *should* slow my life down—another one of my faults."

Lucky chuckled. "Let's just do a little at a time. Don't forget, using lucky words includes how we talk to *ourselves*. You can start with that—and let it be your goal today."

Christopher was still trying to shake off the grogginess of a sleepless night. Wiping the sleep out of his eyes, he said, "You're right. Maybe you can help me stay accountable."

Lucky shrugged. "To me, the best way to help someone is often just to set an example. But I'll encourage you and be here for you whenever you need me."

"If you say so, Lucky. I'll follow your lead."

He grinned. "Terrific. In that case, I'm going to *lead* you to breakfast—in about half an hour. Or . . . do you think you're able to get there on your own this morning?"

Christopher playfully jabbed a finger toward his friend. "Sounds like a challenge to me. Just watch—don't *you* be late!"

"Whoa, look who's taking control of their lucky life this morning!" Lucky laughed and added, "I'll see you in half an hour," then he stood and walked out of the room, gently closing the door as he left.

When Christopher got to the kitchen, Maggie was at the stove, and Lucky was seated at the table reading *The Chattanooga Times*.

"Good morning!" the pair called out in unison.

"Good morning to you both. It's going to be a great day—I can already sense it." Christopher stretched his arms upward and then sat down across from Lucky.

"That's what I like to hear to start the day—positivity!" Lucky put the paper down in a chair beside him as Maggie brought over two plates of scrambled eggs, bacon, and sliced potatoes.

"Oh, that's definitely the breakfast of good luck," Christopher said excitedly, rubbing his hands together.

"You'll need it today—we're going to have a busy few hours," said Lucky.

Maggie chimed in, "You've got to watch out for him, Christopher. Before you know it, he'll have you hiking through the steepest parts of the mountains. He likes to push himself to new levels—a little too fast sometimes, in my opinion." She grinned and set down two cups of steaming coffee.

"She's not wrong," Lucky admitted with pride. "But seeing as you've had a heart attack, I'll cut you a break."

The three of them laughed, then Maggie stepped back over to the stove, rolling her eyes playfully and shaking her head.

Lou reached for his coffee, gave Christopher a wink, and then the two men began digging into their breakfast. After a few seconds of savoring Maggie's cooking, Christopher broke the silence.

"Lou, being here with you and Maggie is so healing for me—and I don't just mean physically."

Lucky put down his fork and listened intently as his new friend continued, "I haven't felt like laughing or even smiling in months . . . but I have here. Thank you."

Lucky smiled gently. "You know, using the 'new' way of speaking with lucky, optimistic words will significantly increase your happiness—and that of people around you. It's really astounding how it works."

Christopher's newfound happiness washed over them as they finished their breakfast. After draining his cup of coffee, Lucky suggested a field trip.

"I know a little place tucked away in the mountains where we can have a picnic lunch and sit and talk for a while. It's tranquil and has a great view."

"I'm with you." Christopher gave him a high five.

Lucky suggested they meet back in the foyer in ten minutes. "We'll drive to the park and then take the trail to the spot I'm talking about. It's not too far, and the fresh air will do you good."

Christopher nodded his approval, and the two headed back to their rooms to get ready for the day ahead. Once they returned to the den, Lucky gave his hiking partner a quick rundown of their morning.

"It's a ten-minute drive to the trailhead. We'll hike for about an eighth of a mile and then take a break before reaching our final spot."

Christopher gave a thumbs up and nodded toward the brown wicker basket Lucky was holding. "Anything else we'll need besides that?"

"Nah, everything we need is right in here." He patted the basket, looked over toward Maggie, who had now entered the room, and thanked her for the lunch.

Christopher added his appreciation, to which Maggie waved a dismissive hand and smiled. "The best thanks you both can give me is to enjoy it."

With that, the two men jumped in Lucky's old truck and headed down the driveway toward their adventure for the day. As they drove along, Lucky pointed out various landmarks and significant historical locations for Christopher to take in.

"That's where the Battle of Lookout Mountain began—also known as the Battle Above the Clouds."

Lucky gestured toward a jagged, brushy area with views overlooking the valley.

"It was one of the most brutal Civil War battles of the South. Hard to believe it happened here when everything is so peaceful now."

Christopher shook his head. "I don't know a lot about the Civil War, except that it was gruesome."

Lucky nodded solemnly. "Hundreds of thousands of people lost their lives. Brothers fighting against brothers—even fathers fighting against sons. I pray we'll never experience that again, or anything like it. . . ."

Lucky's voice trailed off.

"What was it like during the Troubles?" Christopher asked quietly.

"I suppose a lot like the U.S. Civil War," Lucky said thoughtfully. "Friends fought against each other, and communities were ripped apart."

Christopher stared out the open window. "You know, in a way, it's what my divorce felt like. My life with Sarah was blissful for so long. When we finally separated, there was so much anger and disappointment, it felt like our entire world had been split open. We turned on each other—something we never, ever believed would happen."

Lucky nodded in understanding and then pointed up ahead. "We'll pull off here at the overlook and leave the truck. Not many folks know about this place . . . lucky for us!" He guided the vehicle off the narrow road and then parked at the end of the lot, closest to the trailhead.

Christopher stepped out, and his gaze drifted over the valley. "I feel like I can see forever!"

Lou chuckled. "It's a clear day, and supposedly on Lookout Mountain, you can see six states when the weather is like this."

Christopher squinted. "I can see a lot, but I don't know about six states."

"Yeah, probably an exaggeration," said Lucky. "What's there to see in Kentucky, anyway?" He flashed a toothy grin. "Come on, let's hit the trail—I've got the basket."

Christopher followed cautiously behind as they entered the brush area. Lucky pointed ahead at the entrance to an almost hidden path. "It's not used that often since it's not marked, but it's my favorite."

Lucky pushed a pine branch out of his way and held it back for Christopher, who scurried onto the rugged path.

"Watch your step, there's going to be lots of rocks and roots jutting up today which could be, um, *problematic* if you fell in the wrong place."

"Yeah, it's a long way to the bottom, I'm sure," Christopher replied with a nervous laugh.

After fifteen minutes, Lucky nodded toward a large rock just to the side of the trail. "Let's sit here for a quick break."

Christopher wiped his brow and then sat carefully on the boulder as Lucky reached into the basket and pulled out two bottles of water. He handed one to Christopher, who took it gladly.

After several large gulps, Christopher said, "Wow, it's hard to believe it gets so hot and humid this early."

Lucky took a quick sip of his own water and then wiped his forehead. "Welcome to the South, Brother."

But as he smiled at Christopher, something on the trail caught his eye, and he stiffened. Christopher followed his line of sight.

"What's wrong, Lou?"

Then he saw it, too: a snake winding across the trail away from the rock they were sitting on.

"W-what kind of snake is that?" he stuttered, trying to keep his voice even.

"Copperhead, and they're aggressive."

The snake suddenly stopped, turned back across the trail, then slithering slowly toward the two men.

"Don't move," Lucky whispered, and Christopher held his breath as the serpent unexpectedly turned back again and glided off the trail into the woods.

Christopher finally exhaled. "I'm glad I'm with the luckiest man alive," he said grimly. "That thing was probably six feet long! If it had been just me, I—"

Lucky smiled and interjected, "I believe you are about to violate lucky secret number one."

"I guess you're right. Man, this is going to take some work!"

"I'd say you were lucky yourself today, Christopher. A deadly viper crossed your path, and you lived to tell the tale."

"Yeah, but it—"

Lucky held up his hand. "No 'yeah buts,' my friend. Remember, every opportunity you have, find lucky words to use. Alright, let's keep going."

Lucky took to the trail again. Christopher rose cautiously, cast a glance in the direction of the snake's path, and briskly caught up with his friend. The two men continued on for another ten minutes, and then Lucky abruptly stopped.

"Let's turn left here."

Christopher peered to the left. "Um, that's taking us to the edge of the mountain . . ."

Lou stroked his beard thoughtfully and replied, "You're right. Now, let's go." He started off again and then turned and grinned at Christopher, who tentatively followed.

As they continued through woods even less traveled, pushing the tree limbs back in places, they now kept an eye on the ground, watching for more snakes—or any other unwelcome critters.

At last, Lucky stopped, pulled back a large branch, and turned to his friend.

Christopher stepped forward and what he saw took his breath away.

"It's absolutely magnificent!"

Lucky smiled and let the branch go as they eased out to an overlook unlike anything Christopher had seen. Before them was a precipice giving way to a sprawling vista, and to the right, there was a flattened area perfectly suited for two weary travelers to share a meal.

"How did you find this, Lucky?"

"Guess I'm just . . . Lucky." He raised the corners of his mouth.

Here, it was like they had gone back in time. There was quiet all around them, and the valley seemed to stretch to infinity.

Christopher couldn't stop staring.

"Come on, let's sit down and enjoy our lunch," Lucky offered.

He promptly opened the brown wicker basket and pulled out two savory barbecued chicken sandwiches on soft, fresh buns. He reached in again and withdrew a container of baked beans, coleslaw, and two large brownies.

"We'll save these for dessert." He winked.

Lucky spread out a red-and-white-checkered tablecloth, and with that, the pair began their delectable-looking meal. They spoke seldom as they simply enjoyed the food and the marvelous sight before them.

The hikers washed down their lunches with Maggie's sweet tea, and then Lucky packed up the containers, glasses, and utensils.

Finally, Christopher broke the silence. "This is just what I needed. Simple, yet perfect."

Lucky nodded. "Agreed—and you just provided the 'perfect' lead into the second secret of luck:

## "THE SECRET OF CONTENTMENT."

Christopher pushed his salt-and-pepper hair back as the breeze blew gently past the two men. "So, I'm guessing you're going to tell me we should be simple monks, like St. Patrick?" He frowned.

"What St. Patrick meant was, we should be appreciative of wherever we *currently* are in life. All the super-lucky people he met had this mentality that if we have a little, then we should learn to be content with a little. If we have a lot, then we should be content with *that*."

Christopher leaned back against a rocky backstop and crossed his arms in doubt. "Easy to be content when you have a lot."

Lucky wagged a finger at his friend. "I beg to differ. I know people who have more material things and money than they know what to do with, but they're unhappy because they're *always* searching for more. The core of understanding contentment is this: if you're constantly chasing what you don't have, you'll *never* have enough."

Christopher nodded slowly as Lucky continued.

"St. Patrick and the lucky people he discovered were content with whatever was put in their lives. They found and counted their blessings. Even if they had lofty goals, *they were content with having little while they worked toward having more*. In fact, I would say if a person can't be content with a life of simplicity, they won't be content with one of wealth or material success."

Christopher nodded. "I think I see what you mean. Contentment is a mindset." His shoulders slumped, and he stared into the distance.

"What are you thinking?" Lucky asked gently.

Christopher shuffled his feet. "I'm thinking about the times I pushed my daughter to do more, to be more, to want more. Looking back, I never stopped—and I never allowed *her* to stop, and savor where she was. I had good intentions, but maybe this is part of why she doesn't have anything to do with me. There's no way you can enjoy being around someone who makes you feel like you're not enough. I just wish I could tell her I'm sorry."

Lucky nodded, sensing the deep hurt his friend was feeling. "Remember, we don't always know why situations occur in our life, but it's important to trust that there are lessons inherent in each of them. That's where contentment is key."

Christopher exhaled and took in the sight of the valley below. "I understand. Before Lookout Mountain, I felt anything but contentment, and now, my eyes are starting to open to the possibility that things were happening that way for a reason. Still, the pain . . ."

Lucky leaned forward. "Like I said, these lessons are hard to learn sometimes, but learn them we must. Even though there's a lot of pain involved in what you have dealt with, you're going to find contentment will serve you well. It's never too late to learn this lesson."

Christopher sat quietly. "You may be right, Lucky, but . . ."

Lucky broke in again, and a slight smile appeared. "You now have two lucky secrets under your belt. Don't break both of them right now. First, speak lucky words. That means we don't say, 'Yes, but." Second, be content. In this case, trust that the timing is right and be content with where you are in your life at this very moment."

It dawned on Christopher that his mentor's words would permanently impact him. He gazed out over the far-reaching vista and said pensively, "Right now *is* perfect. I feel 'lucky' to be here and to understand what you are telling me—or what St. Patrick's words are teaching me."

Lucky nodded. "I agree." He smiled and joined his pal in taking in the beautiful valley. "I *wholeheartedly* agree."

Just then, Lucky held out his hand as a small, yellow-breasted bird flew toward him. Incredibly, the bird landed in the man's outstretched palm.

Christopher stared open-mouthed as he watched Lucky reach for some breadcrumbs with his free hand and offer them to the winged visitor, which quickly gobbled the morsels.

Lucky smiled and then gently raised his palm toward the sky. "Off you go now!"

The bird flew into the distance, and Christopher blurted out, "Lucky! How did you—?"

Lou cut him off, "When your life is in complete harmony with The Five Secrets, you lose any bit of tension, anger, or selfishness—traits that normally repel others. Even the animals sense it." He smiled. "For example, our relaxed gestures, unhurried breathing, and gentle movements express contentment with our life."

Christopher nodded in shocked silence, then the two men simply savored the land below them.

A few minutes later, Christopher asked, "How did you end up in Lookout Mountain?"

Lucky took a deep breath. "There again, I guess you could say I was just lucky." He laughed. "But, I also believe it's where I'm supposed to be."

Christopher's forehead creased, and he crossed his arms, listening intently.

"When I came to the U.S., I came through New York. I felt at home in the melting pot that is New York City, so I stayed there for several years. Then, I heard from friends about New England, so I took a train north and headed to Connecticut, since I was told it was an especially beautiful place. I ended up in a town on the coast called Groton, and I loved it—maybe because it reminded me of a village in Ireland where my uncle lived. I used to visit him during the summer, and I have so many good memories of those days. . . ."

Christopher nodded his understanding. "I was close to my uncle too. Unfortunately, he passed away not too long ago."

"I'm sorry. My Uncle Stewart passed away fifteen years ago, and I still miss him terribly, so I understand the pain."

After some pensive silence, Lucky continued.

"In Groton, I met a wonderful woman named Becky. We fell in love, married, and stayed in Connecticut for fifteen more years. We had a daughter together, whom I adored."

Christopher's interest piqued as Lucky went on, his voice trembling.

"Then, Becky and I started fighting. As I look back, I realize how petty a lot of the arguments were. Yes, sometimes I was right, but . . . I know now it didn't matter. Back then, I *had* to be right, and I *had* to let her know it. Unfortunately, all of this took place before I had delved into the scroll and its wisdom—and my ego and poor decisions cost me dearly."

Christopher shook his head empathetically. "I had no idea. Our situations sound so similar. I'm sorry, Lou."

"Thank you for saying that. You know, I think many spouses feel the need to always be in the right, rather than be *content* with their partner's opinion. But I couldn't accept, or even value, Becky's opinion. I was young, arrogant—and insecure. Our arguments got worse, and one day I came home to find Becky had vanished. The divorce got processed through our attorneys, and I never saw her again, and even worse than that, I never saw my beautiful daughter, Cara, again. She was only ten at the time, but my wife moved her away, and we've had no subsequent contact—it's been nearly thirty years now, and I still think about her every day. I even heard Cara had gotten married, but I only knew about it years after the fact . . ."

Christopher's eyes glistened. "Lou, I can relate so well to what you're saying. I moved out of our home three years ago, and I've had no communication with my daughter since then. Megan is twenty-one now, and she won't take my calls or return my emails or texts. I'm afraid part of the problem is Sarah has turned her against me, and at this point, there's nothing I can do about it."

Then he scrunched up his face and shook his head. "To not have contact for *thirty years*, though, I can't imagine the pain—but I'm terrified the same will happen to me and Megan." At a sudden thought, he blurted out, "If only you had—"

Lucky raised his hand as if he knew what Christopher was about to say, and he interjected.

"I know. *If only I had had The Five Secrets of Luck to guide me then.*"

Christopher tilted his head. "Well, yes, I was wondering about that . . ."

Lucky shrugged. "As I said, I didn't even unpack the scroll until after the divorce. But as we've discussed, 'bad' things can often end up being some of the best things that happen to us in the long run. Yes, they are painful, but we also don't always know where the pain is going to eventually lead us."

Doubt crossed Christopher's face, which Lou recognized.

"Don't get me wrong. I wouldn't have chosen it to go this way, but not everything is up to me. I simply trust that everything is going to work out. So, I have faith that someday I'll see my daughter again."

Christopher exhaled loudly. "It comforts me to know that there's a bigger plan at work. Even when I feel 'unlucky,' that is not necessarily the case . . . unless I choose to see it that way."

There was pride in his voice as Lucky replied, "Yes, we have the *opportunity* to practice contentment, and we must use our lucky words to frame and then shape each situation. This is how a truly lucky person operates. Can you see how much this would have helped you in your recent circumstances?"

"For sure," Christopher admitted. "The beauty of what I have learned so far is that I have the ability—and the *opportunity,* as you said—to reframe situations as part of my journey toward a happier and luckier way of living. With these two tools, I feel . . . more powerful, somehow."

Lou nodded and then stood, casting a glance once more over the vista. "*Powerful.* Yes, you've chosen an appropriate word. Now, let's start heading home—it's late in the afternoon, and we still have to hike back to the truck. Mustn't overextend you."

"I suppose you're right, Lucky."

Christopher smiled and got to his feet, then the two men gathered their belongings and stepped back onto the trail. As they began their descent, Christopher wondered more about his friend's past.

"Lucky, when did you leave Connecticut?"

The Irishman continued to walk as if he didn't hear the question, but after a few seconds passed, he responded. "About six months after the divorce, I decided I couldn't stay in New England. My wife came from a wealthy family, whose highly-paid attorneys made it impossible for me to see my daughter—and I didn't have the money to keep paying the legal fees. Becky said Cara wanted nothing to do with me, and knowing I couldn't be a part of their lives was too much. . . ."

He shook his head as if to shake the memories.

"I moved out of Groton and came to Lookout Mountain. I kept hearing about how special Chattanooga was, and the Lookout Mountain area especially appealed to me because I was near the city, yet I lived in a quiet, small community. I still love it today, and I have become close to lots of people here."

Christopher pushed a branch out of his line of sight and smiled. "I can tell the people love you, Lucky, and obviously, you feel the same way about them—it must be nice. I remember I used to feel that way about my life in Albuquerque . . . until everything changed."

"I understand what you mean," said Lucky. "Change is hard. However, your two tools of lucky words and contentment are going to be helpful as you move forward—regardless of where you end up next."

Christopher took in the wisdom his friend had shared with him. He had the distinct impression that his time with Lucky in Lookout Mountain had already been life-changing.

As the hikers stepped out of the woods and walked toward the truck, Christopher's mind was reeling. He reflected on what he had learned so far—and what other lessons from the scroll could possibly lie ahead. . . .

# Chapter Nine

The two piled into the vehicle and headed back to Lucky's home, exchanging small talk along the way.

"Tell me something, Lucky—after all these years, do you think about dating someone else?"

Lucky pushed his hair back as the wind blew in through the open window. "Not really. I've got Lep, I have my home, and Maggie takes good care of us both. I'm not sure I really have the need—or the time—for anyone else."

"Well," Christopher admitted, "I'm grateful you were available for me that day in the coffee shop. I can't imagine where I would have ended up." He frowned at the thought, and then added, "The barista, Sam, told me about the difference you've made in his life, too."

Lucky smiled. "Sam is an amazing young man, and believe it or not, he's made even more of a difference in my life than I have in his."

Before Christopher could ask him to elaborate, Lucky turned into the driveway and announced, "Home sweet home! How about we take a dip in the pool and rinse off some of this mountain trail dust?"

"Sure, sounds good," Christopher replied, looking forward to cooling off.

Lou parked the truck and grabbed the picnic basket. Just as the two friends were walking up the front steps, Maggie opened the door, a smile on her face and Lep by her side.

"Well, the hikers have returned!" She took the basket from Lucky and put a hand on Christopher's shoulder to guide him inside.

"A little disheveled," said Lucky, "but we enjoyed our lunch . . . and we made it out alive! We're thinking about going for a swim. Could you—?"

"Say no more," Maggie interrupted. "I'll bring some beverages and snacks out to the pool."

The men looked at each other and smiled, then Lucky turned back to Maggie. "Twist our arms, already!"

After throwing on his trunks and a t-shirt, Christopher walked down to the den and found Lucky waiting with a grin. He gestured for Christopher to follow him.

"We'll just go through the back door, and the pool is off to the left."

Christopher stayed close behind as Lucky led him outside. There were colorful plants, flowers, and even some gorgeous cold hardy palm trees lining the way. They turned a corner, and a full-length swimming pool came into view with multiple sun loungers and even a bar at the other end. The entire area was enclosed by a tasteful wrought-iron privacy fence.

"Wow, this is fantastic, Lou. I'm starting to feel luckier by the minute!"

Lou laughed, and the pair sat down on loungers on either side of a small plastic table. As if on cue, Maggie delivered two glasses of sweet tea, each filled with ice.

"Oh, this is perfect," Christopher crooned. "It's pretty simple to feel content at times like these."

Lucky flashed a toothy grin. "I have to admit, there's not a lot to complain about out here." He held his glass of tea toward Christopher, who picked up his own and clinked Lucky's as the Irishman offered a toast.

"To great days ahead."

"I want to believe that, Lucky." He smiled and took a large gulp of the tasty tea, then slowly reclined in the lounger, feeling the warmth of the sun on his chest. "Lou, are there still times where you feel a little, um, *unlucky* since those days in Connecticut—or have you left that mindset far behind?"

"Your timing is impressive because I was just about to say something about that." Lucky stretched out also and put on his sunglasses. "This is as good a time as any to tell you about the third lucky secret."

Hearing this, Christopher sat up, now donning his own shades.

Lucky began, "One of the most important ideas St. Patrick wrote about was service. The idea of generosity is so deeply ingrained in the secrets, it's almost impossible not to see the work from a perspective of selflessness."

Lucky sat up and then turned until he was facing Christopher. "The third secret is:

## "THE SECRET OF SHARED LUCK."

As the words left his mouth, a strong, cooling gust blew across the pool area.

Lucky gestured to the wind. "It's just like this rejuvenating breeze after a hot day in the woods—kindness and compassion revive us and others. We never know what people's lives are like or what they are going through, and when we consistently fulfill this third secret, something powerfully good starts happening in *our own* lives.

"This is why—to answer your earlier question—I have very few days when I feel 'unlucky.' Each time I get the feeling that life is being unfair to me or that I have been slighted, I take that as my cue to see if maybe I've become too focused on myself. If so, I regain perspective by taking a step back and thinking about how I can help others feel life is better than they realize—maybe even better than mine."

"Even *better* than yours," Christopher echoed pensively.

Lucky nodded. "That's right. Here's how I see it after all these years of practicing The Five Secrets: *Everything* is happening to help us reach our goals."

Christopher rested his elbows on his knees, steepled his fingers, and continued to listen.

"Shared luck is the underpinning of the precepts. St. Patrick and his lucky outliers had embedded it deeply into their daily lives. They knew there was no way to be happy if they weren't focused on helping others feel happier—or luckier, I guess. Thankfully, The Five Secrets teach us how to implement this concept of magnanimous living."

Christopher grinned.

Lucky excitedly pressed on. "You see, this is a major difference between St. Patrick's 'luck' and the modern-day version of it: everything St. Patrick proclaimed had a noble element woven through it. In fact, his main objective in writing the treatise was to help others live better, happier, 'luckier' lives. These days, people associate luck with getting more, making more, and finding more prosperity and material success, with little thought of others. They are missing the magic ingredient—service."

Christopher exhaled. "Of course! It's another thing I've been missing over these years—I have slipped away from a life of service and slipped into a life based on what's only best for . . . me."

A gentle smile crossed Lou's face. "I think you're learning, buddy."

He continued, "Here's a big takeaway, Christopher: If we aren't mindful, we'll spend so much time thinking about how to make our lives better, that we'll forget the secret is to make *others'* lives better. Everyone knows it, but few people can, or will, put it into practice."

With that, Lucky announced, "Time for a break. How about we take a quick dip in the pool? After all this hot air I've been blowing, it might cool us both off a bit." He chuckled.

Lucky got up from his lounger and dove headfirst into the cool water, then emerged and pushed his stringy hair out of his eyes. "Ah, now this is more like it!" He splashed his friend liberally, who then dove in also.

"Relaxing out here is such a great change from back home," Christopher said, treading water. "I had no idea these few days would turn out like this, but I'm so grateful they have. I feel like I've been . . . fighting for my life—even before the heart attack."

Lucky nodded. "It's been good for both of us, Christopher—and we've got more powerful words from our friend St. Patrick to examine soon, so buckle up." He backstroked slowly toward the other end of the pool, a grin on his face.

After enjoying a leisurely swim, Lucky suggested they  get out for a few minutes. Suspecting it had something to do with the third secret, Christopher stepped out of the pool after Lucky, then dried off and reclined back into his lounger. Basking in the warmth of the summer sun, Christopher threaded his hands behind his head, closed his eyes—and promptly felt someone nudge him.

"Don't get too relaxed—I think you'll find this quite useful." Lucky grinned, and Christopher shook himself from his sudden drowsiness.

"Okay, okay, I'm ready."

"Christopher, do you remember the first day I met you in the coffee shop?"

"Sure," said Christopher, "you asked a little about my life and what made me think I was unlucky."

"Correct. What I have shared with you about making *others* feel lucky—don't take it for granted."

Christopher sensed the heaviness of Lucky's words. He took off his sunglasses and squinted over at the Irishman.

"When I told you about Belfast and the day my father and Sean died, I left something out . . ."

Christopher's eyes were now wide.

"For the longest time, I felt their deaths were somehow my fault. Or at minimum, I felt guilty I couldn't have helped more."

Christopher nodded, listening intently.

"They call it survivor's guilt, and that's exactly what I had—guilt for having survived. I just *knew* I could have done something different before or after the explosions. Or maybe, *I* should have died instead."

Christopher sat up ramrod straight. "Lou, no. There was nothing else you could have done. You said—"

Lucky held up his hand. "I know what I said, but still . . . I blamed myself. It wasn't a logical response—it was strictly emotional, and one I couldn't control. But regardless, I held myself hostage to my doubt and regret and responsibility, however misplaced. Those feelings almost carried me away . . ."

With misty eyes, he went on, "Here's what I want you to understand, Christopher. I've come to believe, like you just said, there was nothing I could have done about their deaths. But I've also come to realize that I *can* help others. I can help people feel better about their own lives and relieve some of their doubts, insecurities, fears, and regrets."

Christopher sat quietly as Lucky continued, "After my divorce, I discovered the scroll and delved deeply into St. Patrick's words. I became so committed to the Secrets and to helping others feel lucky that the very act of service started to heal me. Making other people's lives better was—and still is—one of the most therapeutic actions I can take for myself. I'm not fully healed yet, but I'm getting closer."

Christopher said slowly, "When I said earlier that I was 'worrying about me—and me only'. . . on the contrary, you're telling me that it's not only *kind* to serve others, but it is the way to help *ourselves*."

Lou nodded. "Right. It's the essence of The Secret of Shared Luck."

Both men fell silent, reclining in their loungers. After a pensive minute, Christopher spoke.

"Sam the barista told me that meeting you was the best thing that happened to him when he came to Lookout Mountain. I have a feeling you have helped a lot of folks like Sam."

"Gratefully, I *have* been able to help many people," said Lucky, "but many others did not want my help or didn't realize they needed any help. It's about doing what we can, not trying to force anything on anyone. If I force my solution or my assistance on someone who doesn't want it, then I am doing the act for *me*, which is selfish—and there's typically a cost for that."

Christopher nodded. "I guess I didn't know how badly I needed help when we met, and truthfully, I didn't even want it. I had no idea how far I had fallen in this whole 'good luck' game."

Lou shrugged. "Sometimes we don't realize how much our perspective has become corrupted—it happens so gradually that we often aren't even aware of it. Yet once we're at rock bottom, it becomes extremely difficult to dig ourselves out of the hole, so to speak."

Christopher nodded vigorously. "Yes, I can vouch for that."

"But," Lucky added, "there is almost no greater alchemy than when 'unlucky' thoughts change to 'lucky' ones. It produces a subsequent snowball effect in a person's life."

He glanced down at his watch. "No wonder I'm getting hungry—it's almost six o'clock!"

Christopher's gaze fell to his own watch. When it did, a distant look appeared in his eyes, which Lou immediately picked up on.

"What is it?"

Christopher shook his head. "I'll talk with you about it at dinner." He quickly tucked his watch into a small bag next to his chair, as if he wanted to avoid seeing the time. It was 5:59 p.m. . . .

# Chapter Ten

Christopher took his time getting ready for dinner after he returned to his room. He showered and read a few chapters of a book he had brought from Albuquerque, before returning to the dining room at 7:30.

Once there, he sat down in the same chair as the night before, across from Lucky. Maggie brought two glasses of white wine, and after they thanked her, she left for the kitchen to put finishing touches on the night's meal.

"I trust you're feeling better?" Lucky asked as the two raised their glasses and tasted the wine. "I've noticed your smile has gotten bigger since you've been here."

Christopher gave a mirthless laugh. "I'd almost forgotten how to smile."

Lucky shook his head. "Smiling is essential for a lucky person. Not much can make you unluckier than constantly wearing a frown, or even a stoic countenance."

Christopher scoffed, "It's really that important? Come on, Lucky."

"People have so much on their minds, they often don't realize they look grumpy," said Lucky. "Worse, they appear unapproachable, and they'll certainly miss out on opportunities to raise their spirits—or improve their lives."

Christopher rubbed his chin. "I remember after the divorce, I was feeling horrible about myself. No doubt my countenance screamed 'I'm unhappy'—mainly because I *was*." He managed a half smile. "I remember a customer of mine once asked if I was angry with him. What's ironic is that it wasn't him at all—I was angry with . . . *me*."

Lucky nodded and went on, "Even if we feel like we're putting on a false front when we 'fake' a smile, we don't know how badly someone else may need that look of affirmation."

"Plus," Christopher added, "whenever I smile at someone, it tends to make *me* feel better, and more often than not, they'll smile back at me."

"Yes, a perfect example of facilitating shared luck." Lucky smiled and then changed the subject. "Christopher, I noticed that you cringed when you glanced at your watch earlier, around six. Care to tell me about that? You don't have to, but . . ."

Christopher took a long sip of wine, and began: "A couple of years ago, when I was in the thick of all this misery, and my stress level was through the roof, I was on my way home from work . . ."

He paused, but Lucky encouraged him.

"Take your time."

Collecting his thoughts, Christopher continued, "It was late fall, and the days were getting shorter. I was on a two-lane highway near my home just after dark. I came to a light in the road—a blinking yellow light. I needed to cross the highway, and I looked and saw it was clear, but when I turned, there was a tremendous crash—I can still hear that crunching metal. A vehicle coming from the opposite direction had hit me nearly head on."

Trying to keep his voice even, Christopher finished, "The driver didn't have their headlights on, and I never saw them. It was completely unexpected—and terrifying."

Lucky palmed the back of his neck. "Christopher . . . it must have been horrible. Was everyone okay?"

"We were both hurt, and our cars were demolished. When the state patrol arrived on the scene, they were astounded there were no major injuries or deaths. Traffic was backed up after that for an hour as the ambulances and tow trucks arrived. When the trooper wrote up his report, the time he listed was . . . 5:59 p.m."

Christopher gulped and continued. "The accident traumatized me, and for a long while after, I had a hard time driving at all. Plus, even though the other driver's lights were off, I was deemed at fault, which led to other problems."

Lucky steepled his fingers and leaned in, listening carefully as his friend finished.

"It was one more example of how life seemed to have it in for me—or at least, that's how it felt. Now, whenever I see that fateful time on a clock, I just . . . freeze for a moment."

Both men sat in silence as Christopher's words hung in the air. Finally, Lucky spoke. "I'm sorry. I can tell you've suffered—and greatly. I'm glad you're here to heal."

Christopher raised his head and said quietly, "Me too, Lucky. Thank you . . ."

A few solemn moments later, there arrived a cheerful distraction in the form of Maggie, laden with their dishes: fried chicken, French fries, macaroni and cheese, and other tasty Southern favorites.

"Maggie here has won more than her share of blue ribbons in the Dade County Fair food contests. Her food is not just excellent—it's *spiritual*." Lucky beamed.

Maggie, humbled by the praise, waved her tea towel at Lucky playfully. "Oh, he doesn't want to hear all that!"

Christopher held up his fork and smiled broadly. "I'll tell you this, Maggie: if you ever open a Southern restaurant, I'll be your first customer!"

The woman blushed, then turned and walked gleefully back into the kitchen as the gentlemen continued with their feast. After another two hours of eating and talking, Lucky glanced at his watch.

"Well, that was another wonderful meal, but I think we should turn in. You've got that early morning appointment at the doctor for your checkup—it's been a week."

"Wow, I can't believe it—seems like only yesterday." Christopher shivered at the memory of that day at the coffee shop. "And we've only known each other for a little over a week, but it feels like I've known you forever."

Lucky grinned. "We meet the people we need to meet to learn the lessons we need to learn. You're doing very well so far."

Christopher stood. "Thank you. I hope I'll get a good report tomorrow from the doctor as well."

Lucky got to his feet and cast a knowing glance at his new friend. "You're going to get a great report. When you do, I've got a little surprise for you. Well— more of a *big* surprise."

Christopher tilted his head.

"Sleep well," Lucky said with a wink before leaving the room.

Christopher turned and saw Maggie standing in the doorway, having overheard Lucky's mysterious comment.

"Any idea what the surprise is?" he asked.

"Guess you'll find out tomorrow," she replied with a smile.

Christopher smiled back and headed to his room. He was eager for a good night's rest, and he was now astoundingly confident in what would come from the doctor's report tomorrow.

Christopher stretched his arms wide, and his lips curled upward as he woke the next morning to a colorful Lookout Mountain sunrise. He was pleased to be feeling grateful for the view, as opposed to sad while seeing the sunrise at the inn mere days ago. The longer he stayed with Lucky, the more he believed his life was somehow getting better—and it felt like a *miracle*.

A few minutes later, there came a knock on the door and Lucky's deep, mirthful voice.

"Room service!"

Through the slightly open door, a hand appeared holding a large cup of steaming coffee.

Christopher reached out and opened the door the rest of the way. "Ah, thank you, my good man," he replied, accepting the cup. "I would certainly tip you, but I'm a little short on cash." He grinned.

"Yeah, yeah, that's what they all say." Lucky's eyes crinkled.

"We've got about half an hour until Maggie has breakfast ready. After we eat, we'll head into town to see our friend the doctor."

"To get my good report—and my subsequent surprise," Christopher added with a grin, then taking his first sip of coffee.

"Correct. See you soon." Lucky smiled and shut the door on his way to the kitchen.

Shortly after they finished breakfast, the two were on their way to the doctor's office. It was only a ten-minute trip, and once they arrived, the men stepped inside just as the nurse was calling Christopher's name.

"Mr. Stone, are you ready?"

Christopher winked at Lucky and then walked over to the woman.

"Ready as I'll ever be." He added with a sly grin, "In fact, I'm kind of excited because I *know* it's going to be good news."

"Now that's the kind of optimism I wish all of our patients had." With that, she ushered Christopher down the hall to the exam room.

Half an hour later, nurse and patient reappeared in the waiting room. She spoke a few words to Christopher, then smiled at Lucky before calling her next patient.

Christopher walked over to his friend and exhaled loudly in relief. "The doctor said he couldn't believe how well I've already recovered—he'd never seen anything like it!"

Lucky patted him on the back. "Wow, that's great news!"

"And he said I could do anything I'd been doing before—within reason, of course." Christopher beamed.

"I should have known—you had that lucky attitude about you when you walked into the office, so how could you *not* get a great report?" Lucky's eyes sparkled and he added, "Come on, let's go to the car. I think it's time I share some more good news with you."

They walked to Lucky's waiting truck. Once they got in and buckled up, Lucky eased out of the parking lot in the direction of his home.

"So, now that the doctor says you're officially back in the game, here's what I would like to propose . . ."

Christopher looked at him expectantly.

"I think we should take a trip."

Christopher's eyebrows shot up. "What kind of trip?"

Lucky took one hand off the steering wheel, then reached over and gently clasped his friend's shoulder. "A trip to Belfast."

"Wait, what?" Christopher couldn't contain himself. "Like, just you and me?"

Lucky shrugged. "Well, you said you've had it on your bucket list, so, yes."

"Lou, I'm not sure I can afford that right now. I mean, with the divorce, and all the other expenses I have, I just—"

Lucky held up his hand to stop him. "All of that will be taken care of—don't give it a second thought."

Christoper ran his fingers through his hair and leaned back. "That would be a trip I'd always remember."

Lucky smiled. "More than you realize. You have two more Secrets of Luck to learn, and the best way I know to teach you is to take you to the Old Country. There are people you need to meet in Belfast. We'd be gone about a week, and I know once you've finished your time there, you'll have a new way of looking at life.

"So, what do you say? Shall we go 'across the pond?'" Lucky stuck out his hand.

Christopher smiled, and without hesitating, reached and shook his friend's outstretched hand. "I can't think of anywhere I'd rather go, or any person I'd rather go with."

Lucky put his free hand back on the wheel, grinning. "I knew you'd say yes. We're booked on the flight from Chattanooga to Belfast tomorrow morning at 8:00 a.m. Let's get home and start packing!"

The rest of the day was spent preparing for their trip. The weather in Belfast would be much cooler than in Lookout Mountain, so Christopher needed to pack accordingly.

"Hey, are we going to run into any leprechauns while we're there?" he asked Lucky, who had stopped by the guest room to check his friend's progress.

"Of course not." Then he smirked and added, "But maybe a few trolls and elves . . ."

Christopher guffawed. "I really can't believe we're headed to Ireland. Thank you, Lou."

The older man waved a dismissive hand. "You're going to learn so much there. Like Maggie said about her picnic lunch, 'The best way to thank me is to enjoy the trip.'" He smiled.

Before Christopher could respond, Maggie appeared in the doorway with crossed arms. Lep was beside her, wagging his golden tail.

"I distinctly heard my name mentioned—and Lep agrees." She raised an eyebrow and grinned.

"I was just sharing your philosophy about enjoying life," said Lucky. "Christopher is starting to get the hang of that idea, I do believe."

Maggie nodded. "Well, I have certainly learned a lot from Lucky about living a happy life."

Christopher's interest was piqued. "Oh yeah, like what?"

"Well, there's just *so* much," Maggie gushed. "But if you're learning about living a lucky life, the most important thing he's taught me is that it's not life's problems that make me feel unhappy or unlucky—it's my attitude toward those problems. Lou helped me develop a new, constructive mindset about everything that happens to me. *No one* can convince me now that I'm not lucky. And to think I used to believe there was a black cloud hanging over my head!"

Christopher nodded and raised his hand. "Yep, guilty."

She chuckled nervously. "Lucky helped me realize that my black cloud had a silver lining. It was just up to me to find it. I didn't realize I had been getting some kind of odd satisfaction from drawing attention to my problems—or my perceived problems."

Lucky glanced pointedly at Christopher. "Yes, we talked about that idea also, Maggie."

She went on, "Well, once I started focusing on all the possibilities, everything changed. I must admit, I was at my wit's end—I had so much sadness and regret."

Lucky smiled at her. "Ah, but then tell Christopher what you discovered . . ."

She nodded. "Yes, then I discovered I had the ability to start with a clean slate and reimagine my life. With Lucky's help, I started believing things were going *right* for me. I finally started believing . . . in myself and my God-given abilities."

She held up her hand to stop herself. "Anyway, there's plenty more, but suffice it to say, my life has not been the same since I met Lucky and he shared the Five Secrets with me. You'll learn like I did, trust me." She smiled and added, "But now, it's time for dinner, gentlemen. I've fixed some special dishes for you."

"Sounds good, Maggie," said Lucky. "See you in a few minutes in the dining room."

She smiled warmly, then turned and walked off to put the finishing touches on their final meal before their departure.

Ten minutes later, during their dinner of Cornish hen, roasted potatoes, sauteed green beans, and fresh tomatoes, the two friends talked excitedly about their upcoming visit.

"So, what exactly are we going to be doing in Belfast, Lucky?"

"That's part of the fun—I'll tell you when we get there. Just know that we've got lots to see, lots of people to meet . . . and lots to learn to get you ready for your official debut at the lucky club." He winked.

After finishing their meal, Maggie served a delicious homemade chocolate pie. Then, following a little more conversation, the pair stood, thanked her, and went their separate ways to get a good night's sleep before their long flight to Belfast.

When the driver arrived at five a.m. the next morning, Lucky and Christopher were waiting for him. They each had only one suitcase to load in the car since Lucky had insisted they pack simply. "Remember, a lucky person's life is about contentment, and simplicity is a close relative of contentment—so we must pack lightly," he had said with a grin to his travel partner.

They piled into the shiny black limousine, and they were off to the Chattanooga airport, about thirty minutes away. The chauffeur, Ollie, had driven Lucky on many other trips previously.

"How long will you be back in the homeland, Lucky?" he asked with a smile.

"Only a week, Ollie. Wish we could stay longer." He reached up and patted the man affectionately on the shoulder.

"Guess you're going to load up on luck while you're there, huh?"

Christopher chuckled and pointed toward his friend. "I don't know how much more luck this guy can hold!"

The three laughed together, and the conversation flowed just as easily for the rest of the short trip. Once they pulled up to the curb at the departure terminal,

Ollie walked around to let the men out, then grabbed their luggage for them. "See you both soon. Want to just give me a holler when you're headed back, and I'll come pick y'all up, Lucky?"

"Sounds like a plan!" Lucky answered. He tipped the tall, slim man generously, and then the travelers walked into the airport to begin their departure process. About forty-five minutes later, they heard the call come over the intercom.

"Chattanooga to JFK, departing at Gate Eleven in one hour." The men, who at that point were finishing up a quick snack, heard the announcement and promptly paid for their meals so they could get in line to board.

Reaching their gate, the reality of the trip they were about to take dawned on Christopher. "This is so exciting, Lucky. Going to New York, then to Belfast . . . nothing better than travel, huh?"

The corners of Lou's lips turned up. "I'd say we're pretty *lucky*, wouldn't you?"

Christopher nodded. "Oh, incredibly lucky, I'd say." He smiled back.

With that, the two men handed their boarding passes to the agent and stepped onboard to begin their journey.

Christopher Stone's life was about to change forever. . . .

# Chapter Eleven

It turned out to be a slightly delayed two-hour flight to New York, and the travelers had just enough time to catch the connection to their final destination, which proved to be a comfortable, yet uneventful segment.

Once on the ground in Belfast, Christopher was taken aback by the beauty of the Irish countryside surrounding the airport. The lushness, the variety of flowers . . . it all reminded him of Lucky's home on Lookout Mountain.

When an approaching skycap grabbed their luggage and offered to take them to a cab, Lucky agreed, but the man's Irish accent was almost impossible for Christopher to understand.

"Um, Lucky, did he say something about a taxi? Clearly, he's not from Albuquerque." He chuckled.

"Careful," Lucky replied under his breath, "I think he might be a leprechaun."

Both men burst out laughing, but the skycap just raised his brim, none the wiser.

"Here you are, gents. The taxi will take you to Dunadry Castle."

Lucky pressed some coins into the skycap's palm. "That's perfect. Thank you."

Christopher's jaw dropped. "Did he say . . . *castle*, Lucky?"

"That's right. How else are we going to find Gavin O'Grady unless we go to his castle?"

Christopher leveled his eyes at Lucky. "Who in the world is Gavin O'Grady?"

At that moment, the skycap, who had been about to leave, stopped and turned toward Christopher—and this time, his words were perfectly clear.

"Who is Gavin O'Grady? Well, he's only the luckiest man in Northern Ireland!"

Lucky raised an eyebrow and added, "Maybe in the world, wouldn't you say?"

"Most likely!" The worker grinned.

The driver tipped his cap and began loading their luggage into the cab as Lucky and Christopher jumped in and buckled up.

"Off we go," he said cheerfully, maneuvering the taxi into the airport traffic.

Christopher took advantage of the quiet car ride to gain perspective on where he now was.

"Ah, it's so beautiful—and there are sheep *everywhere!*" he exclaimed.

As they continued down the highway, the driver pointed out various landmarks. Occasionally he would add an eyeroll and say, "And look—*more* bloody sheep!"

Christopher belly-laughed. "So, I guess everyone in Northern Ireland is used to all the sheep, huh?"

Lucky shrugged his shoulders and laughed with him. "Yes, it's like kangaroos in Australia or monkeys in India—you just get used to them. They become pesky little rascals."

"So," Christopher asked, "who is Gavin O'Grady?"

"He's my mentor," Lucky replied. "I met him before my mother passed away."

Christopher nodded in interest.

"I'll let him finish the story when we get there." Lucky pointed in the distance. "There's the turn to go to the castle."

Christopher craned his neck to see. "We're really going to a castle, huh?"

"Yes, just outside Belfast, and you'd better act civilized—Gavin doesn't put up with any nonsense." Lucky gave him a half smile, and Christopher didn't know what to make of this information.

When the cab turned at the sign for Dunadry Castle, in the small town of the same name, it was only about two more minutes until they arrived at their destination. The driver stopped at the stone guardhouse, then spoke a few sentences in Gaelic to the man there, who waved the vehicle forward.

As they headed down the winding drive, Christopher shook his head in awe. "I have to say, it's just like the pictures I've seen of Irish medieval castles."

He pointed ahead at a water-filled moat over which lay a drawbridge. After passing over it, the car pulled up by the castle's massive wooden front door.

The driver opened each of the men's doors and tipped his cap. "Dunadry Castle, lads."

Christopher looked on in awe at the imposing medieval stone structure. "It's incredible!"

As if on cue, the residence's door creaked and swung open, and a handsome, fit butler with slicked-back black hair appeared.

"Greetings, gentlemen!" Then his lips curled up. "Mr. McGraw, it's a pleasure to see you again."

Lucky reached out and gave the man a hearty hug. "Ah, I never tire of being here—and it's been way too long. When was my last visit . . . five years ago, Winston?"

The servant nodded. "You are precisely correct, Sir."

Lucky turned to see the cabbie standing patiently beside their luggage, so he walked over, thanked the man, and handed him two pounds. The driver offered his appreciation and, after sizing up the castle, stepped back into the cab to head out on his next trip.

Lucky rejoined his party. "Winston, this is Christopher, from America. He's my new friend, and I thought we'd let Gavin spin some tales for him."

The butler nodded and smiled. "He would love that, I'm sure, sir. Do come in, gentlemen." He ushered them inside before picking up their luggage and following them, closing the heavy wooden door behind them.

As soon as they crossed the threshold, a tall, lean man—likely in his early seventies—with a full head of tousled grey hair approached. He didn't speak, but instead looked the two visitors up and down.

He turned sternly to the butler. "You just let anyone in here these days, don't you?"

Christopher chewed on his lip nervously, but the man guffawed and reached out to Lucky in a warm embrace.

"Lou! You old scoundrel—it's about time you made your way back here," he said, patting Lucky heartily on the back. "You know, I'm getting to the point where you just can't be away for five years and expect me to still be alive when you come back to visit!"

Lucky chuckled as he pulled away. "Yes, yes, sorry, my friend. I'll do better next time."

He turned and gestured toward his travel partner, who was visibly relieved. "Gavin, I want you to meet my friend Christopher Stone. He's come all the way from Albuquerque, New Mexico, to listen to your nonsense." He smiled widely.

"Well, I'm full of that, for sure." He reached out to Christopher and clasped his hand firmly. "Glad you're here, Christopher. It's always a treat when Lou brings along a friend because I know they'll have an interesting story."

Christopher shuffled his feet and deflected. "I'm not sure you'll be interested in my story."

Gavin paused and looked toward Lucky, who shrugged.

"Hmmm, I'm guessing somebody either hasn't been taught St. Patrick's first secret, or they haven't had quite enough time to let it sink in." He smiled.

Flustered, Christopher palmed his forehead. "The Secret of Lucky Words. Yes . . . as you can tell, I'm still working on that."

Lucky jumped in. "He's making good progress—it's just taking a little time. That is why, my good mentor, we have come to see you." He opened his palms. "After all, who better to reinforce The Secrets of Luck—and to teach the final two—than you?"

Gavin bowed humbly. "Of course—the final two secrets have changed my life forever. But we'll talk more about that another time. Why don't you gentlemen let Winston show you to your rooms? When you've settled in, we'll meet in the courtyard for an afternoon tea and a chat."

Winston quickly took charge of the suitcases and motioned with a nod for the men to follow him. Once they reached their rooms, which were up two flights of wooden stairs and at the far end of the hallway, the butler gave them parting instructions.

"Mr. O'Grady will meet you in one hour, which will give you a few moments to rest and unpack. Mr. Stone, the courtyard is through the den and to the right, then out the back door."

Each of the men thanked the butler, who then turned and took the creaking staircase back down. Lucky waved to Christopher, and both men disappeared inside their rooms.

As he unpacked, Christopher looked around the spacious room and noticed the many classical paintings, which he assumed dated back hundreds of years. Some subjects appeared to be knights, and others were gentlemen dressed in perfect-fitting suits with British top hats.

Exhaustion and jet lag finally catching up to him, Christopher groaned as he lay down on the four-poster bed. It was a spectacular, hand carved cherry frame, and the bedding was soft and thick. Nestled in a sea of pillows, he closed his eyes and found himself dozing off as he wondered what his time in the castle with their jovial host would hold. . . .

After what seemed mere minutes, Christopher heard a tapping on his door. He jumped up, rubbed his eyes, and stepped over to open it.

"Lucky! What time is it?"

Lucky grinned. "Relax, it's only a few minutes before five. I had a feeling you might be asleep, so I thought I would come get you."

Christopher thanked him. "Give me a moment— I'll just change my shirt and meet you at the bottom of the stairs."

Lucky nodded and shut the door. In a few moments, Christopher had splashed some water on his face, put on a fresh shirt, and was out of his room. He walked quickly down the stairs, and upon reaching the main floor, he saw Lucky turn his wide-eyed gaze up after checking his watch.

"I think you just set a castle record!"

Christopher chuckled, and the two men made their way to the courtyard to meet Gavin. Crossing the ground floor, Christopher was astounded by all the antique decor.

"These things look like they're from the Middle Ages!" he breathed.

Lucky broke his stride and replied evenly, "They are."

"I know you're used to all of this," said Christopher, "but . . . I'm blown away."

Christopher was equally impressed once they reached the outside area. Opening the door was like entering the portal to a different world. Christopher looked from one side of the massive garden to the other. The variety of flowers was stunning—they were not like the stiff, spiky plants he was used to in Albuquerque.

After a few seconds, he spotted Gavin in the distance, sitting under a magnificent stone gazebo at an oval wooden table with a white tablecloth. Beside him was an elegant tea service in silver. As he and Lucky approached, their host stood and Winston appeared out of nowhere to gesture toward their seats. Gavin then nodded for the butler to pour the tea.

"Milk and sugar?"

Both visitors agreed, and Winston then dispensed the tea into all three cups, bowed slightly, and disappeared again.

Gavin took a sip of tea. "How do you like my little place?" he asked, fixing Christopher with a piercing gaze.

Christopher gestured at the castle and around the gardens. "If you will allow me to say so, Gavin, you're a lucky man."

The host set down his tea slowly, with particular precision. "Well, yes, I am a lucky man. But that would be true whether I lived in a small shack—which I have—or in this magnificent castle. Comparison is the thief of luck, you know." He picked up his tea again and sipped.

Christopher nodded. "Yes, Lucky—er, Lou—taught me about contentment . . . Lucky Secret Number Two."

Gavin smiled, but then Lucky jumped in.

"Christopher, there are a couple of things I want you to understand. First, the reason I wanted you to visit with Gavin is that he lives out the Five Secrets of Luck unlike anyone you'll ever meet."

Gavin nodded to his friend. "Thank you, Lou."

"But secondly," said Lucky, "I owe Gavin a lot . . . maybe even my life. May I?"

He looked at his mentor, who nodded his approval. Christopher leaned in.

"After my father and Sean died, I was devastated—as you can imagine," Lucky said. "My life went into a tailspin, and at one point, I just didn't know if I could handle everything."

Gavin hung his head, remembering, as Lucky continued.

"My mother had heard about Gavin, who at that time was a priest. She reached out to see if there was anything he could do to help. He immediately came to visit me, and . . ."

Lucky hesitated as his eyes became moist.

"It wasn't anything he said. It was more like his presence, his nonjudgmental attitude, his unwavering belief in me. Something in me changed that day."

Lucky's eyes lit up, and he raised his chin. "After that, Gavin stayed close to us. He's still a dear friend and mentor of mine to this day."

Christopher shook his head in awe, then turned to Gavin. "So, how did *you* learn The Five Secrets?"

Lucky laughed and leaned back. "Yeah, tell him!"

"Well, since you asked . . ." Gavin smiled and began, "As Lou said, I was a priest for most of my life. I had heard rumors of the scroll and St. Patrick's Five Secrets, and although most people doubted the scroll's existence, I believed in it. I immersed myself in learning what I could about the secrets—and in trying to locate the relic, but to no avail.

"When Lou was back in town for his first visit after the divorce, he revealed he was in possession of the scroll. Of course, I told him he was out of his bloody mind." He smirked.

Lucky held up a finger. "Which some people still believe about me." The men laughed in unison.

Gavin added, "Later on, as I pored over the scroll, the secrets resonated with me in a way that transformed me."

Christopher shook his head. "Unbelievable."

Lucky chimed in. "It might sound that way, but it was not just synchronicity—it was divine intervention that brought us together. Gavin was meant to have the scroll in his life. As I mentioned, he lives out the precepts at a unique, highly spiritual level, which I can only aspire to do. His life isn't just lucky—it's borderline *supernatural*."

"Simply by adhering to The Secrets?" Christopher wondered.

Lucky smiled at Gavin and then turned his gaze back to his American friend. "He seldom deviates from them, and consequently, he has developed sage-like qualities."

Christopher exhaled loudly. "So . . . how did you end up here in the castle?"

Gavin raised his shoulders. "Well, believe it or not, that's a less exciting story. It's been in my family for generations—almost six hundred years, in fact."

Lucky nodded. "Dunadry Castle is like a second home to me—I have spent a lot of time here over the years. Gavin was also influential in my decision to go to America after my mother died. He knew I wanted to leave Ireland but just couldn't muster up the courage. Looking back, it was the best thing I've ever done, but it was also one of the *hardest* things I've ever done."

"The hardest things in life often yield the biggest rewards," Gavin remarked evenly. "I knew he would be successful, and I believed America was the best place for him to thrive. Luckily, I was right."

Christopher nodded. "That was fortunate for me, too. I'm grateful to have met Lucky." He exchanged a meaningful glance with his friend.

Gavin clapped his hands together. "Agreed. Now, let's talk about the Secrets. What exactly have you learned so far?"

Christopher held up a finger. "Secret number one, THE SECRET OF LUCKY WORDS."

Gavin nodded. "Go on."

Christopher held up another finger. "Number two, THE SECRET OF CONTENTMENT."

"Right. And . . . ?"

Now he was holding up his first three fingers. "And number three, THE SECRET OF SHARED LUCK. That's all I know so far."

Gavin smiled. "Excellent. Sounds like ol' Lucky Lou has steered you in the right direction. Now it's time for number four—a lovely precept."

Christopher leaned forward, but Gavin paused.

"Before we get into this . . . you said I wouldn't be interested in your story. What made you say that?"

Christopher took a deep breath. "I don't know how much Lou has told you about my situation . . ."

Gavin took another sip of tea. "A little. He said he felt you were a perfect candidate for The Five Secrets."

Christopher ran his fingers through his hair. "Well, over the last few years, I've had some terrible things happen in my life."

Gavin shrugged. "As have we all."

His response rattled Christopher. "But—"

"You just violated Lucky Secret number 1."

Christopher stammered, "Well I, um, never thought I would have to deal with all the situations I am having to . . ."

Gavin held up two fingers. "You just violated Lucky Secret number 2, regarding contentment. Feeling entitled to a *perfect* life is incompatible with leading a lucky life."

Gavin paused, perhaps to see what effect his words would have on Christopher before he changed tack. "That is," he added, "unless you would consider what most see as an imperfect life to be *perfect* to you. Now *that* would be a very lucky philosophy."

Christopher was now visibly flustered, and he looked over at Lucky for support.

Lucky wagged a playful finger at him and said, "Whoops."

Gavin patiently continued. "In this case, the third time is definitely *not* a charm, so don't blow the next one, my New Mexican friend." He winked.

Christopher felt the heat rising to his face along with a pang of embarrassment. "Right, sorry."

Gavin smiled and waved a dismissive hand. "Here's something important to remember about these secrets: they *will* change you. They have transformed me, they have transformed Lou—they are infallible. But you must practice them relentlessly. Every time you catch yourself breaking a secret, you must correct yourself quickly. If you do that, your mind will start course-correcting *before* you violate the secrets."

Christopher nodded, and Lucky then cut in.

"I know from personal experience that what Gavin is saying is true. It's not like I instantly embodied the secrets. It took time, but as I continued practicing, they sank in and became a part of my life out of habit."

"That's another thing I have struggled with: patience," Christopher realized aloud. "If you asked my daughter, I'm sure she would tell you it's one of my weaknesses, and it always has been. I guess it's just my nature."

Gavin spoke up. "Be careful when you talk about your 'nature.' Each time you say that, you are taking away your personal power. You're effectively establishing your limitations. Even if something feels ingrained, it can be overcome—but only if we start with affirmative words, or '*lucky* words.'"

Lucky nodded in agreement.

Christopher smiled. "Words create our circumstances, right?"

Gavin replied, "Yes, but there's more—which brings us to the fourth, and my favorite, secret:

## "THE SECRET OF LUCKY PERSPECTIVE."

"It's my favorite, too," Lucky affirmed to Christopher.

Gavin nodded. "I love it because this secret reminds me I have control over my life. Anything that happens, good or seemingly bad, makes me stop and ask myself, *How is this situation going to benefit me?* And I always find an answer from that perspective. The more I look for proof that I'm lucky, the more proof I find. But, most people inadvertently look for proof that they are *unlucky*—and they find it, too."

"Why would people do that?" Christopher asked.

Gavin raised his shoulders. "I don't know. But folks constantly complain about how bad things are going, how difficult their lives are, how unfair everything is—and before you know it, they're right! They find their life is difficult, people are rude, circumstances are painful, and it just gets worse. I think it's what Einstein was referring to when he said, 'The only question we must answer is, "Is the universe friendly?"' Once we decide that, we have laid out our path. Life is either our friend . . . or our foe."

Christopher grinned. "Or, in St. Patrick's terms, life is either lucky or unlucky."

Lucky smiled and playfully jabbed a finger at Christopher's chest. "Exactly!"

Gavin nodded his agreement and continued. "I learned that St. Patrick practiced this concept constantly, maybe even more than all the other secrets. When he was in captivity, he kept telling himself there was a reason it was happening. He believed that all the suffering was leading him to something bigger in life—which of course, it was."

Lou gestured with his teacup toward his American friend. "This secret is not for the weak. Like St. Patrick, I have practiced it consistently—the result being that I believe everything is happening for my benefit. Since I *truly* believe that, others believe it about me, too."

"'Lucky Lou' McGraw," Christopher mused. "No wonder people in Lookout Mountain think you're lucky—because in your opinion, only good things happen to you. Kind of like being 'grateful for everything.'" He beamed.

Lucky's eyes sparkled. "I do believe you're starting to understand this whole idea of 'real' luck, aren't you, Christopher?"

"Yes, I just wish I had known it before . . ."

Gavin held up his hand. "Again, that's the point, Christopher—you *didn't* know it then. You made choices based on the information you had at the time. Now, you have different information, and you'll make different choices. There's really no failure when you look at it like that—just learning."

"*Just learning*," Chrisopher echoed. "That's so freeing."

Gavin clapped his hands together enthusiastically, then leaned back and chuckled. "Yes, isn't it? And what's more, you get an infinite number of chances. It's not like there's some great universal clock, ticking away on your decisions. All that is asked of you is to forgive yourself when you make mistakes, learn from them, and move on to the next situation in your life—with that acquired knowledge."

Christopher sat in amazement, taking it all in. He couldn't believe everything he had learned from Lucky and the first three secrets already—now, this fourth one was crystallizing his understanding even more.

Gavin broke through his thoughts, announcing, "Gents, I'm getting a bit peckish, as we say here. Why don't we talk more over dinner in the city? I think you'll enjoy seeing part of Belfast, Christopher, and I have some reservations for us at my favorite restaurant."

"That sounds perfect," Christopher said gratefully. "I'm ready—and I'm hungry, too."

As if on cue, Winston arrived and announced, "Your car is here, sir."

Gavin thanked the man, then they all stood and walked through the gardens to the front of the residence to catch their ride into town.

# Chapter Twelve

Once they were on the road, Gavin—who sat in front with his trusted driver, William—acted as tour guide, pointing out the highlights of historic downtown Belfast along the way. "There's the primary school I attended. I still ache every time I remember the nuns hitting my knuckles with a ruler when I was a boy."

"Ouch!" Christopher winced, rubbing his own knuckles.

Shortly after that, the chauffeur pulled off to the side of the street just ahead of a small restaurant. "The Laughing Lamb, sir."

"Excellent, thank you, William." Gavin patted the man's shoulder. "Pick us up around nine o'clock?"

"Absolutely, sir. Enjoy your dinner, gentlemen."

The three passengers stepped out of the car and walked to the front door of the restaurant nestled between storefronts of grey stone. A husky, middle-aged man dressed in a navy suit and a crisp, green bow tie opened the door and ushered the diners in.

"What a pleasure to have you back with us tonight, Mr. O'Grady—and we welcome your friends."

"The pleasure is always mine, Stewart." He shook the man's hand enthusiastically, and Christopher watched Gavin place a fifty-pound note in his hand.

The maître d' then stepped forward, greeted the three men, and led them to a quiet table in the back. Christopher took in the fine Irish linen tablecloths, and then his view rose to the dark paneled walls with drawings of castles and large manors.

"What a fantastic place," Christopher breathed.

"Yes, The Lamb has been here for over three hundred years," said Gavin. "It's a private establishment with excellent food, but without 'stuffy' patrons—hence you'll see a variety of attire, though the staff is dressed formally. My father used to bring me here; his father used to bring him . . . and it has been the same with other families for generations."

As they were seated, the waiter greeted the men cordially and set in front of each of them a cocktail without an order having been placed.

"The Gavin Special, sirs—Jameson, plus a touch of strawberry, the national fruit of Ireland." Gavin grinned broadly as each of the men held up their glass and toasted the day—and the fact that Lucky and Christopher were visiting.

"It's always a pleasure when Lucky comes to town," said Gavin after they had each taken a sip. "Our discussions run the gamut, but of course, my favorite is about The Secrets."

Lou nodded in agreement.

"By the way, Christopher," Gavin added, "I want to revisit our earlier discussion. I had asked why you said I wouldn't want to hear your story . . ."

Christopher searched for the right words. "It's just a tale of a bad luck streak."

"Give me an example," Gavin pressed as he took another sip of his cocktail.

Christopher recounted the story of the car accident, occasionally glancing at Lucky, who encouraged him in the telling. When he was finished, Gavin was looking Christopher up and down.

"Are you okay?" Gavin asked him pointedly.

Christopher's mouth twisted. "What do you mean?"

"Well, you don't seem to still be hurt—it sounded like a terrible accident."

"It was."

"Then I would say you were pretty lucky not to have gotten injured or killed."

"Well, I guess . . ."

Gavin held up his hand. "You are *definitely* lucky."

"He's got a point, Christopher," said Lucky.

Gavin leaned back. "It's *the* point. This is exactly what St. Patrick was talking about when he said that lucky people look for proof they are lucky."

Christopher's brows drew together. "But who would actually believe I was lucky after something like that?"

"Who cares what anyone else thinks!" Gavin blurted out. "As I said, the more you follow the Secrets of Luck, the more *you* will start to believe you're lucky. Consistency is key when it comes to living out the secrets. Eventually, others will see it too—though, their recognition of your charmed life should never be your goal."

At that moment, the wait staff approached their table with several dishes, which had been ordered ahead of time by Gavin. It seemed to Christopher there was enough to feed ten people! He marveled at the varied choices of Irish stew, roast chicken, steak, corned beef and cabbage, bowls of colcannon, and baskets of soda bread.

"This is incredible, Gavin. I can't believe it!"

"Please, enjoy," Gavin replied warmly. "I love making sure my guests get plenty to eat while they are here."

"Well, so far, so good," the New Mexican replied with a grin.

The men enjoyed their meal and conversation for over an hour and a half before the server came and asked for any final requests. Gavin looked around the table, and the others waved their hands dismissively.

"I'm stuffed, Gavin." Lucky shook his head as he pushed his chair back.

Christopher held his hands up. "I give up, too. I couldn't eat another bite."

Gavin appeared pleased, and as he asked for the check, Christopher raised a finger and offered to help, which Gavin immediately declined.

"Not on my watch, lad." He smiled broadly.

The three gentlemen then stood to leave, and as they walked out, Gavin shook hands with nearly every person in the restaurant.

Lucky turned to Christopher and whispered, "Lucky people make other people feel lucky—as you now know. Gavin is a master at that, and it's always genuine. It's why he's loved wherever he goes."

Christopher nodded, and the trio piled out into the cool night air, finding William already parked out front for their return trip.

He greeted the passengers as they slid into their seats. "How was the meal, gentlemen?"

"Just perfection," Christopher gushed. "Plus, I felt like we had the mayor at our table tonight. Gavin must know everyone in town!"

"Some would say Mr. O'Grady knows everyone in *every* town in Northern Ireland." He winked in the mirror at his passengers.

Christopher leaned forward and asked, "Do you really think you're lucky, Gavin?"

Without hesitating, the older man exclaimed, "Of course I'm lucky! Each day on this earth is a divine gift, and I get to live out the principles of St. Patrick every day. I live a life of complete trust, and when you live by trust, new opportunities arise all the time."

Gavin paused and steepled his fingers.

"Everything we've talked about today leads to the mindset and attitude of feeling lucky. At this point in my life, I can assure you everything that happens is leading me toward a happier, richer, even luckier life. I would be foolish to think otherwise."

Christopher countered, "But don't things ever go wrong for you—I mean, *really* wrong?"

Gavin sat quietly, and Christopher wondered if he had upset him. After a few seconds, Gavin replied, "Everyone has things go wrong. Take Ernest Hemingway, for example—I saw you reading a book of his at the castle. Aside from his tragic end, would you call his life lucky?"

Christopher shrugged. "From what I've heard, I'd say most of his life was charmed—or at least, it appeared that way. He traveled the world, wrote incredible books, and enjoyed a life of luxury most of us could only envy!"

Gavin shook his head. "Did you know Ernest Hemingway was in two plane crashes during his travels in Africa? In fact, he survived those crashes *on back-to-back days*."

Christopher gulped.

"Now, would you consider that lucky—or unlucky?"

No one answered.

"It's *all* perspective, my friend. I'll bet Hemingway would say he was incredibly lucky, while others would say he was incredibly unlucky."

Christopher nodded. "Okay, I see, but—"

Gavin cut in. "Speaking of perspective—and plane crashes—what about Juliane Koepcke? In 1971, at seventeen years old, she was the lone survivor on a plane that crashed into the Amazon after being struck by lightning. She spent ten days in the jungle before she was found alive."

Christopher's eyes widened. "Wow, wasn't *she* lucky?"

Gavin rubbed his chin. "I don't know . . . *was* she?" He continued, "Some would say lightning striking your plane and causing it to crash is incredibly *bad* luck. Others would say she was incredibly *lucky* to have survived."

Christopher pondered the story. "Hmmm . . . I guess it's a matter of perspective, just like you said."

"Precisely."

William pulled off to the side of the road as a police vehicle approached from behind. With an uneasy feeling, Christopher watched as it stopped directly behind them, and two officers jumped out and tackled a man running down the sidewalk.

"Stay put, everyone," Gavin warned his group.

As the officers turned the man over, one reached under the perpetrator's coat, and a woman's purse tumbled out, its contents sprawling across the sidewalk. The policemen quickly cuffed the man and stood him up, then placed him in the back of the squad car.

Lucky shook his head. "Parts of Belfast have become really dangerous, haven't they?"

William nodded, and Gavin replied, "Yes, it's become a daily occurrence here—the muggings, the thievery. Best not be out on the street at night in many areas of the city, sadly."

Lucky added, "What a shame . . ."

Gavin gave a subtle nod, and William pulled the vehicle slowly back onto the street. Moments later, a majestic cathedral came into view, illuminated against the darkening sky.

"That is Saint Anne's Cathedral, a special place I once visited as a child," Lucky said with a touch of nostalgia. "It was built in 1899, and my understanding is it's become not only a spiritual gathering spot, but a cultural hub as well. I still vividly remember my visit, even though it was nearly sixty years ago. In fact . . ." His voice trailed off.

Gavin looked back at him and smiled. "What is it?"

Lucky shook his head and grinned. "It sounds silly, but one of the items on my bucket list is to hear a sermon in the cathedral."

Christopher was impressed. "*Any* sermon?"

"About the power we have to make a difference in the world. To hear that message in the magnificence of the cathedral . . . yes, that's what I want to do." He nodded and smiled at the thought.

Christopher's face brightened. "Well, if you were using lucky words, you would say, 'One day very soon, I will be in that great place, and I will hear a sermon about changing lives.'"

Lucky arched an eyebrow and smiled. "Touché, my friend."

There was silence in the car for several seconds, then Gavin spoke, carefully measuring his words. "This is what people don't understand when they use the term 'luck' loosely. Everything we have talked about today is built on faith. So, for people to believe they can shortcut the process and somehow be given a life of random good fortune is just *nonsense*. Not only that, even if they could have a genie grant them that wish of luckiness, they would miss out on the beauty of the process. They would not be part of the learning, the growth, the aha moments that make the discoveries so wonderful."

"Yes," Lucky agreed, "and I'll bet St. Patrick would have said the same. He surely didn't enjoy the hardships he endured, but I'm sure he would not have traded the lessons for anything. You can't have growth without pain of some sort, and gratefully, St. Patrick passed those lessons of growth on."

*You can't have growth without pain.* It was such a simple concept, but it was suddenly profound to Christopher. That was exactly the phrase he needed to hear. All the suffering he had endured over the last five years . . . it had all brought him to this moment. The pain of separation from his daughter, the accident, the business struggles, the divorce, the heart attack . . . all the stress he had dealt with had brought him to Belfast, Ireland, into the presence of these two men of greatness.

Suddenly, as they passed the cathedral and it got smaller in the rearview mirror, Christopher Stone felt a sense of gratitude, freedom, and peace that he hadn't known in years. As he leaned back, the other passengers seemed to recognize his need to reflect, and there was silence for the rest of the trip.

Sweet, gentle, comforting . . . silence.

When the group arrived back at the castle, it was around ten o'clock, and everyone was ready for a good night's rest. They thanked William, and Gavin encouraged Christopher and Lucky to come down for breakfast at their convenience the next morning.

"I know it's been a long journey, so rest well. Tomorrow we'll spend the day up at Giant's Causeway on the north part of the island. Once there, I think you'll agree it was worth the trip. Plus, there's the little thing about learning that fifth and final secret." He grinned.

Lucky smiled at Christopher, who returned the gesture and then thanked his host for the day. "I'll look forward to tomorrow, Gavin. I've heard lots about Giant's Causeway—and of course, I can't wait to learn the final Secret of Luck."

The men went their separate ways for the evening, and when Christopher reached his room, he climbed right into bed. He was exhausted from the day, but he also wanted the night to pass quickly—like a child eagerly awaiting Christmas morning. He couldn't imagine what gifts the next day would bring. . . .

# Chapter Thirteen

Christopher awoke around seven thirty. Though he tried to get more sleep, it eluded him, so he moved to a small woven chair by a window. He reflected on Lucky's story about the agony of being separated from his daughter, Cara. He marveled at how his friend was able to rise above the pain in a noble commitment to help others grow through *their* pain.

Looking out the window, his mind went back to Albuquerque . . . and to his own daughter.

He wondered what Megan was doing. Did she ever think of him? Christopher never could have imagined that one day, he would no longer have a relationship with his own daughter. As she was growing up, he'd gone to every dance recital, every school play, every sporting event . . . whatever Megan did, Dad was there.

But well before the divorce, things had started to fall apart—not only with his wife, but with his daughter as well. Sarah had made sure to tell Megan the side of the story she wanted her to hear, and the tender-hearted, impressionable girl had believed every word.

Sure, some of it was true, though he had tried so hard to be a great father. But work had slowly gotten in the way as he grew the business, convincing himself it was what he *had* to do for the family. When he realized more money meant much more time away from home, he felt so torn and unsure of the right course to take. Then there were more arguments, less trust, less listening, less sharing, and more stress. The fear of failure became like a noose, relentlessly tightening around his neck, slowly draining him of the life he once cherished. Before he knew it, his family was distant, and then broken.

Christopher hung his head, tears flowing as he stared out over the grounds of the castle. Even with the beautiful view in front of him, all he felt was unshakable sadness.

A knock on the door startled him, and Christopher snapped out of his thoughts and leaped to his feet. Pivoting and walking toward the door, he wiped his eyes and wondered if it was Lucky again.

He placed his hand on the knob, opened the door slowly, and found himself face-to-face with Winston, behind whom stood an impatient young man with a brown messenger bag at his hip. He was dressed in navy jeans, an old grey T-shirt, and a baseball cap, and appeared annoyed the butler was accompanying him.

Winston spoke first. "I'm sorry, sir. He insisted this needed to be put directly in your hand, so I escorted him up here and—"

The messenger butted in. "Are you Mr. Stone?"

Christopher replied slowly, "Um, yes . . . ." as he reached to grasp the large, beige envelope the courier was handing him. "May I ask who this is from?"

The man shrugged. "I'm just the delivery guy." He laughed, but then added, "I *will* say it's from America, and like your friend here said, I was told to deliver it directly to you."

Christopher's eyes narrowed as he peered at the handwriting on the envelope. He thanked the deliveryman, who tipped his cap and was promptly escorted back downstairs.

Christopher closed the door and crossed the room to his seat by the window. Then with a creased brow, he opened the packet and withdrew the single page inside.

*Dear Christopher,*

*I know you weren't expecting to hear from me, and I'm sure you're wondering how I even found you. Well, it's a long story, and it's not important. But what is important is . . . I wanted to tell you the doctors say my life is coming to an end.*

Christopher's hands shook as he continued.

*Several months ago, I found a lump in my right breast. I didn't panic, because I hoped for the best . . . and you were always so optimistic, I thought I would try to be more like you. Unfortunately, it turned out to be worse than was originally thought, and the doctors gave me only three months to live. By the time you get this, I will likely be gone.*

Christopher leaned back and exhaled loudly as he dabbed the moisture from his eyes. It took him a moment to clear his vision enough to keep reading.

*I know it's odd for me to reach out after all we have been through, but I wanted you to know I'm sorry we couldn't make things work, and I apologize for my part in our divorce. Especially during this time, I've been able to more clearly see and understand myself . . .*

*I also know how kind your heart is, and I have no doubt you will feel guilt and regret when you find out I'm gone. If I am right about that, you need no forgiveness from me. I know now you did your best for our family, and I wish I had understood it sooner.*

*One more thing, Christopher . . . Megan loves you. Don't give up on her. I know she has been distant, but she has also been confused and hurt, and she desperately wants you back in her life. I will admit, I did little to help with the way she felt toward you. I deeply regret that and ask your forgiveness. I can only say I was lonely and felt left out of your life, even though now I see things differently. Since my diagnosis, I have asked for her compassion for not supporting you more. I have also assured her that you love her very much and that you two will eventually work things out.*

*In closing, I want to thank you for doing all you knew how to do to make our family work. I am only sorry that we will never go back to our little Magnolia Inn—or any of our other special places—and give ourselves the precious gift of another chance.*

*Goodbye, Christopher . . .*
*Love,*
*Sarah*

Christopher swallowed the lump in his throat and stared blankly at the note. He felt so many things . . . such sadness, but also *redemption*, or at least some relief from the horrible burden he had carried. For Sarah to say she understood and valued him . . . it was really all he had wanted to hear from her. He knew he wasn't perfect. He knew he had made mistakes. But her words would help heal him, and he was so grateful.

Holding the wrinkled, tear-stained letter, Christopher lifted his gaze to the cloudy Irish sky . . . and sobbed openly.

After ten agonizing minutes, the alarm clock broke the silence. Christopher crossed the room and pressed the button gently to end the shrill beeping. He then walked to the bathroom, turned the shower on, and stepped in with the conscious decision to rinse away his past.

Just then, there was another knock on the door.

Christopher cut the water off. "Who is it?"

"Hey, it's Lucky. Just checking on you. Meet me downstairs in half an hour?"

"Perfect, Lucky. See you then."

Minutes later, Christopher stepped wearily out of the shower and began getting ready for his day of travel. His mind was still reeling as he put on his clothes—a pair of light blue jeans and a beige T-shirt blazoned with LET'S GO!

With heavy feet, he marched himself downstairs to the dining room table where Gavin and Lucky were waiting with a hearty breakfast of potato bread, poached eggs, and black pudding—an Irish sausage delicacy.

The two men did not miss the puffiness under Christopher's eyes.

"What's going on?" Lucky asked in a gentle tone.

Thinking it best to get it over with, Christopher told his friends about the letter from Sarah.

"I'm sorry," Gavin offered solemnly.

"Should we take the day off from our trip?" Lucky suggested. "Yes, I think that would be . . ."

Christopher waved a dismissive hand. "I'd like to go. When I got the letter, it was as if I was being told, 'You're almost ready to begin again.' I'm not sure it'll be as simple as that, but I have a feeling our trip today will be an important part of the process of letting go."

Gavin nodded gently, and Christopher swore he saw him almost smile. The sage then took a sip of coffee and repeated Christopher's words aloud. "*Letting go. Hmmm . . .*"

With the weight of the news, the three men finished their breakfast in silence and then were on their way north to Giant's Causeway.

Lucky drove, and Gavin filled the role of navigator, having given William the day off so the group could have plenty of privacy on their journey. The trip was about an hour and a half, and it was up the scenic motorway M2 out of Belfast. Along the way, the trio was entertained by gorgeous Irish landscapes and unusually perfect weather—in the mid 70's—a welcome change from the baking heat back in Lookout Mountain.

Upon arriving at Giant's Causeway, Gavin gave Christopher a moment to take in the breathtaking beauty of the popular coastal area. Formed by historic volcanic activity, forty thousand interlocking hexagonal columns of basalt lay in the distance, rising out of the sea.

As they parked and then stepped out of the car, Gavin pointed ahead to a pedestrian swinging bridge about a hundred feet above the Irish Sea, and a hundred yards long.

"That's the Carrick-a-Rede Rope Bridge that connects the mainland to the small island of Carrick-a-Rede," Gavin explained. "We'll cross the bridge and then walk about half a mile to the left. A friend of mine owns a little cabin there that's tucked away from all the tourists. He said he'd have the fridge stocked for us so we can make ourselves at home and talk. There's a magnificent view over the sea there, too."

"I've been to the cabin, and it's a special place," Lucky affirmed to Christopher. "I think you'll like it."

The men crossed the bridge easily, although Christopher looked down a few times at the crashing waves and had to look back up quickly.

"I've never walked over a bridge like this. I feel like I'm in an Indiana Jones movie."

He laughed nervously, and Lucky chuckled. Christopher glanced at him and noticed how smooth and unhurried his gait was.

"Do you *ever* hurry?"

Lucky shrugged and grinned. "Why would I do that? Rushing causes mistakes, which would only slow me down in the end."

Christopher could only give a nervous smile back in his direction, not least of which because he was too busy keeping his footing.

"Plus," Lucky added, "the resulting anxiety from hurrying would be at odds with the Secret of Contentment."

"Well, I can't argue with that," Christopher managed to say. "Speaking of which . . . do you ever *argue?*"

"Nah, that's usually a waste of time—and it would violate The Secret of Lucky Words."

"Hmmm . . . I see."

"Well, not yet, but you will." Lucky grinned again and pointed ahead—the end of the bridge was getting closer.

Once the men crossed to the other side, they marveled at the massive cliffs and the lush, green fields all around. Stepping onto a well-worn path, Gavin led them through another meadow, then down a gentle slope, with their small lodge now coming into sight.

When they reached the cabin, Gavin unlocked the wooden door and motioned for Christopher to step inside ahead of him. The fact that the little cabin was perched on a majestic cliff made the place even more dreamlike as he crossed the front room and gazed out the kitchen window. His jaw dropped when he observed the waves lapping against the spectacular basalt stones and the rocky shore below.

"It's surreal—I've never seen anywhere like it."

Gavin smiled broadly. "There *is* no place like it. They say you can sometimes see Scotland from here, although I never have. But I think it's the perfect place for us to be today—especially with your epiphany that it's time to start over."

Gavin pointed to a beautiful hand-carved table and chairs in the center of the room.

"Have a seat, gentlemen, and I'll grab us some refreshments. Coffee, tea, or Guinness?"

"Coffee, please," Lucky and Christopher agreed in unison.

Gavin quickly brewed three cups. He set the steaming coffees on the table, then pivoted to open the window, allowing the sound of the sea to fill the room.

"Listen . . ." Gavin cupped his hand to his ear as he sat down with his friends. "It's the sound of life. The waves come in, crash against the cliffs, and they return to the sea, only to come back and crash again. The world is the same way. Life will never be calm all the time, just like the sea. But since we know the waves will crash, we also know that life will go on after that. The tide will recede . . . eventually."

Christopher nodded. "It's true. My father used to say, 'When something troubling happens, it's like a hand being plunged into a bucket of water.' The water is disturbed, but soon, it goes back to being calm."

Gavin pointed playfully. "That, my good man, is a perfect segue into St. Patrick's fifth secret:

## "THE SECRET OF LETTING GO."

Christopher's eyes swung from Gavin to Lucky and back. "Well, this is timely!" he laughed.

"It most certainly is," said Gavin with a knowing smile. "As you spoke at breakfast this morning about letting go, I exchanged glances with Lou, and we both knew the timing couldn't be better for you to hear this secret.

"Fully letting go is the final stage," he went on. "It's the manifestation of a life of trust. The masters of this secret are able to let go even to the point of letting go *of the thought* of letting go."

Intrigued, Christopher set down his coffee and listened as Gavin described the final secret.

"When the going gets tough," he began, "lucky people know they can count on one thing—life will always go on . . . until it doesn't. St. Patrick believed letting go of trying to *force* outcomes was critical, because there were many times he didn't have control. But he also knew, because of his faith, that he could surrender . . . life would continue and eventually bring him to the place he needed to be. Each of the lucky outliers he met deeply believed in this philosophy of living."

"I understand," said Christopher. "Most of my life I have held on so tightly, sometimes literally, thinking I could dictate all the outcomes. But what I have come to believe from being with you and Lucky is that if we simply surrender the results, we can focus on things we *do* have control over."

Gavin threaded his fingers together and leaned forward. "Yes, when we learn how to let go, we learn how to truly live. It's called faith." He smiled.

The men sat in silence as the waves crashed far below their open window.

After a minute, Gavin spoke to Christopher. "Can I warm up your coffee?" He gestured to the still full mug.

"Guess I've been so busy taking this all in, I barely touched it. Yes, please."

Lucky cut his eyes toward his mentor and reached for Christopher's cup. "I've got it."

Gavin nodded as Lucky held the mug on the table between his hands. After a few seconds, he relinquished his grasp and turned to Christopher. "That should be better. Try it."

Christopher's bewilderment did not go unnoticed by either of the other two men.

"Go ahead, taste it," said Gavin, "But be careful—he's pretty good at that."

Christopher tentatively picked up his cup and took a slow sip. His eyes grew large as he blurted out, "It's hot! How'd you do that?"

Lucky chuckled. "I learned it from a friend of mine I met on a trip to India years ago."

Christopher was still awestruck. "That must've been *some* friend!"

Lou gazed longingly out the window. "Yes, Maya was special. I lost track of her after I left India, but she had highly-evolved spiritual abilities—much like those who impeccably live out the Five Secrets of Luck."

Christopher scratched his chin. "Maya . . . I feel like I've heard her name before."

Lucky waved his hand. "I guess you could say . . . that's another story." He grinned. "But what I just did with your coffee is simply an example of our capabilities when we're living a life of *total* trust."

"It's magic!" Christopher gasped.

Gavin wagged his finger in firm correction. "It's nothing of the sort. As I said before, it's faith—and it's a manifestation of unshakeable adherence to The Secrets. But this level is very difficult to attain. St. Patrick and the others did it, and I would say Lou and I have come close, yet we are still novices in the big picture."

Christopher hesitated and then spoke thoughtfully. "I believe I'm starting to put the pieces together. When we embody The Five Secrets, our lives become a representation of deep, unshakable trust. That trust frees us of fear, doubt, and selfishness, and allows us to tap into our capability to do things or be things we would have never been able to do or be before—the 'charmed' effect."

"Yes, that's right." Lucky smiled, laced his fingers behind his head, and leaned back. "Christopher, St.

Patrick's Five Secrets are uniquely powerful, but what do you think happens when we *don't* follow them?"

Christopher tilted his head. "I'm not sure what you mean."

"The way St. Patrick lived was special, yet think about what his life would have been like if he *hadn't* been content, if he *hadn't* consistently looked for proof of being lucky, and if he *hadn't* tried to make sure others felt gifted and uplifted? Also, what if he used *unlucky* words?"

Gavin crossed his arms over his chest, watching and listening to see how Christopher would respond.

The New Mexican paused for a moment and decided, "I suppose he would have often felt miserable, hopeless, and unlucky. But not only that, he would also have spread his negative attitude wherever he went. He probably wouldn't have been capable of doing any of the powerful things he did."

"Precisely," said Lucky. "He would have been just like most people—anxiously trying to stay one step ahead of what they fear. Gratefully for all of us, St. Patrick chose wisely."

Christopher nodded. "You could say St. Patrick was able to 'let go' and let his story write itself."

Gavin chimed in. "That's right—and by doing that, it freed him mentally and spiritually to live in a way that was compassionate and courageous. Letting go softens our energy, which allows us to enter a state of otherwise untapped power." Gavin shrugged and added, "He knew things were going to be okay. Like you said, he knew the water would return to being still."

Christopher echoed the words. *"He knew things were going to be okay."* His eyes darted back and forth between the two wise men. "I see now I have spent most of my life—especially these last few years—trying to *keep* things from happening. Now I see that I should have trusted and *allowed* things to happen . . . I should have let go."

At that moment, a soft Irish Sea breeze blew through the window, and the men relished the feeling on their skin. It was as if a new life for Christopher was being ushered in.

Finally, Gavin's words pierced the silence. "I believe you will look at life differently from now on, Christopher. I can see it in your eyes—you grasp the truths which have been laid out for you."

A tear trickled down Christopher's cheek. "Gavin, you're right, and yes, I'm ready to see my life in a totally different way."

The three men stood, and Gavin's eyes crinkled as he turned to Lucky. "Our work here, as they say, is done."

# Chapter Fourteen

The trio tidied up the cabin, then stepped out the front door, heading to the bridge and eventually back to their car. As they walked, they chatted more about The Five Secrets of Luck, but more than anything, they extolled the beauty of their surroundings.

Once on the bridge, Christopher found it suddenly much easier to cross.

Gavin must have noticed because he said, "It's hard to be in a place like this and not feel improved spiritually. Whenever I come to Giant's Causeway, I leave feeling just a little . . . different."

Christopher shook his head and grinned. "I feel a *lot* different."

The men reached the car, and this time, Gavin volunteered to drive while Lucky took the passenger's seat. Christopher settled into the back, and all three men buckled up for their journey home.

The mood was jovial. Back on the road, Christopher noticed Lucky writing in a spiral notebook.

"Summarizing today's session with your new lucky friend?" Christopher teased.

Lucky rolled his eyes playfully. "Not quite."

He held the notebook up so Christopher could see. "It's called my List of Good. Every day I add three 'good' things about my life. Could be people, places, possessions, experiences—anything goes. Remember secret number four about lucky perspective?"

Christopher nodded. "Look for proof that we're lucky."

"Correct. I started keeping track about ten years ago, and I now have over nine thousand entries. Every time I pull out this notebook and see the abundant goodness in my life, it has a powerful, positive effect on my perspective."

Christopher smiled. "I think St. Patrick would give you extra credit for that one."

Gavin grinned and then offered to the group, "We'll be arriving in Belfast around seven, so what do you say we head downtown once more for dinner? I know quite a few good spots."

Lucky gave a thumbs up, and Christopher rubbed his hands together. "Perfect!"

An hour later, when they had reached a restaurant Gavin knew, there were no spots out front.

"How about if I drop you two off, and I'll go find somewhere to park?" Gavin suggested.

"Sounds good," the others agreed in unison.

Gavin pulled over to the curb to let them out, then pointed in the distance. "It's called The Leprechaun's Delight, and it's just a block down there. If you want to get started walking, I'll catch up with you."

As the car rolled away, Lucky and Christopher started down the sidewalk. While they walked, Christopher reflected on their journey together with excitement.

"Lucky, I just can't believe everything has 'unfolded' like this. I never would have dreamed coming to Lookout Mountain would lead me to you, The Five Secrets, and then to Gavin, here in Belfast. The coincidence is mind-boggling."

Lucky shook his head. "Remember, it's all part of a bigger plan—at least, that's how a lucky person would see it."

Christopher playfully smacked his forehead. "How many times is it going to take for me to remember that there are *no coincidences* for a lucky person!"

Before Lucky could respond, there was a loud *flap-flap-flap* of footsteps as a young man with his face mostly covered by a black bandana came sprinting past them, almost knocking them over. Just as the runner got ahead of the pair, he reached out toward a woman who was walking with a friend, snatched her purse, then unsuccessfully attempted to grab the handbag of the other.

The horrified women shrieked in unison. "Help, police! THIEF!"

With horror, Christopher saw the robber reach under his belt and unsheathe a large, black-handled knife.

Raising the weapon, the assailant barked, "I'll shut you up, you—!"

Before Christopher even knew his friend had left his side, Lucky had reached the man and lunged for the knife. The thief thrust the blade toward the two women's upheld hands, but Lucky's interference deflected it—and it plunged directly into the brave man's own chest.

Lucky winced, staggered briefly, and fell to the ground.

Suddenly panicked at the scene he had created, the now wide-eyed mugger retracted the knife, dropped the purse he had managed to grab, and fled.

The women covered their mouths in horror as Christopher tried to comfort his friend, while a pool of crimson spread slowly across the sidewalk.

"Lou! No, no, no . . . please stay with me!" Christopher screamed in anguish as his friend seemed on the verge of losing consciousness.

At that instant, Gavin arrived at a sprint. Shaking, he knelt beside Lucky and then turned to Christopher.

"I had just parked, and I saw the guy running down the sidewalk toward you. I yelled to you both, but I guess you didn't hear me over the traffic." He shook his head dejectedly.

A police car pulled up and screeched to a stop. An officer jumped out and said, "We caught the bloke just after it happened. My partner was right down the street—he saw him on the run and was able to tackle him."

He crouched to examine Lucky, and then put his hands gently on Christopher and Gavin's shoulders. "Tell your friend to hang on. An ambulance is on its way."

The officer stood and turned to the traumatized women. "Are you ladies okay?"

One of the women managed to speak, though haltingly. "Only . . . because of the man lying there. He . . . he saved our lives."

Her friend nodded, tears streaming down her face. "The guy had a knife—and this man, this hero, came out of nowhere. He didn't even care about his own safety . . ."

The police officer shook his head somberly just as they heard sirens coming around the nearest corner. An ambulance pulled up, and as the paramedics rushed over, Lucky managed to slowly, painstakingly raise a closed hand toward Christopher.

"Take it."

Christopher's eyes grew wide—in Lucky's fist was the silver four-leaf clover keychain from that first day at the coffee shop in Lookout Mountain. The keys were missing.

With shaking hands, Christopher reached for the keychain.

Lucky managed a faint smile. "It's yours, my friend."

"Lou . . . no. You're going to be okay. Lou . . ."

The Irishman gently shook his head. "This time with you was exactly what I hoped it would be—the beginning of healing in *your* life, and the final healing I needed in my own. Welcome to . . . the lucky club."

Lucky winced, then his eyes closed slowly. The paramedic who was taking his pulse paused, shook his head, then turned to Christopher and Gavin. "I'm sorry. He's gone."

Christopher stared at the silver keychain in his trembling palm. Eyes swimming with tears, he turned the clover over, and it was then he saw the Biblical inscription:

*There is no greater love than to lay down one's life for one's friends.*

Christopher slowly lifted his gaze to Gavin, who was now shaking his head in utter disbelief. . . .

# CHAPTER FIFTEEN

"There's just . . . so much to do in three days." Gavin sat at the castle's kitchen table with his elbows propped up, his head resting in his hands.

Christopher absentmindedly swirled his evening tea, which had long since become lukewarm. "I know, it must be overwhelming."

"Thank you for agreeing to help. I don't know how I'd do it without you, Christopher."

"Of course. I realize how *lucky* I am to have met you both, and to learn The Five Secrets. It's the least I can do."

Gavin managed a half smile. "The venue is taken care of. The priest at St. Anne's is a friend of a friend, and I'm grateful he allowed us to move their schedule around a bit. I've also contacted the florist, and hopefully I've remembered everything else."

Christopher nodded and placed a reassuring arm around his friend. "You're doing good, Gavin. Lucky would have loved the service you've put together."

Gavin shook his head. "I just never thought it would end this way."

"I know," Christopher said. "I have so many questions . . . I just have to believe Lucky would not want his life—or its ending—to be any different. One thing I know from my time with him is that accepting the world and our circumstances is key to happiness and good luck." He paused and then added gently, "Of course, that's also straight out of St. Patrick's scroll."

Gavin arched his eyebrow. "You're becoming quite the expert on the Five Secrets of Luck."

Christopher waved a dismissive hand. "Not at all. But I'll get there, because I see things so differently now. . . ."

Gavin smiled and stood. "Let's turn in for the night. I have a feeling tomorrow is going to be a long, difficult day."

Christopher returned the smile, and both men headed to their rooms to get a good night's rest.

Back in his suite, Christopher reminisced on the short but incredibly rich time with his friend Lou McGraw.

He remembered arriving in Lookout Mountain as a shell of a man, and then fortuitously stumbling into the coffee shop.

*"You do seem kind of unlucky."* Christopher turned his gaze heavenward and smiled as he thought about how far he had come since hearing those words.

Yet he couldn't get rid of the nagging feeling that Lucky had gotten "ripped off." *How could such a lucky man who had devoted himself to impacting others' lives be so tragically and abruptly taken from a world that needed him so badly?*

Christopher shook his head, then stepped into the bathroom to start getting ready for bed. He brushed his teeth, washed his face, and put on his pajamas. A few moments later, he plopped himself on top of the covers and lay there with his hands laced behind his neck, staring blankly at the ceiling.

Within seconds, tears began flowing down the cheeks of the weary American as he closed his eyes and tried to block out the deep pain.

When he awoke the next morning, Christopher hadn't budged from the position he had fallen asleep in. Even his hands were still laced behind his head— although they were now tingling.

He stood, shook out the numbness, then crossed the room to the castle window. As he gazed out over the magnificent grounds, it was as if he could hear Lucky's deep voice echoing through the property and across the hills in the distance:

*"Press on, Christopher. Life has great things waiting for you. Just watch . . ."*

Swallowing hard, Christopher pivoted to the bathroom and turned on the shower. He reveled in the feeling of the warm water cascading over his tired body as the steam rose around him.

He stepped out a few moments later and began dressing for the service. As he was lacing his shoes, there was a knock at the door. For a second, he thought it was Lucky, until he realized with a heavy heart it couldn't be. Christopher rose to his feet and opened the door to find Winston holding out a large cup of coffee.

"Thanks, Winston—I can't tell you how much I need that." He managed a smile and reached for the steaming cup.

The man bowed, then gestured to a shiny silver cart behind him. "Your breakfast, sir."

Christopher grinned. "Wonderful—but what about Gavin?"

"Mr. O'Grady has gone ahead to the cathedral, and he said he would meet you there at noon. The service begins at one o'clock, but this will give him plenty of time to bring you up to date on any plans for the day. William will take you to the venue."

"Thank you, Winston. I'll see you when I come down a little later."

The butler bowed again, and Christopher closed the door, eager to examine what was on the cart. He raised the silver domes and admired the delicious homemade breakfast of poached eggs, bacon, soda bread, and fruit. It didn't take long before he had devoured it all.

After breakfast, Christopher grabbed the brown leather journal he had written in during the trip. He wondered how his newfound knowledge about The Five Secrets of Luck would serve him—and help him serve the world. He wondered how things would change, and he pondered where his life would take him. Oddly enough, he wasn't fearful of the future like he had been before meeting Lucky. No, he was excited to now "let his story write itself."

Still, as grateful as he felt, Christopher couldn't stop asking himself why it had turned out this way for Lucky Lou McGraw . . .

# Chapter Sixteen

When they arrived at St. Anne's Cathedral, Christopher thanked William, then stepped out of the limousine. Right away, his gaze lifted to the magnificent, towering steeple. The whole place was stunning, and he thought back on the night he, Gavin, and Lucky had driven past it. He recalled his friend's nostalgia and words of praise for the church—as well as his desire to return someday . . .

His thoughts were interrupted by someone calling his name.

"Glad to see you, Christopher!" Gavin stepped forward and smiled.

He shook Christopher's hand and then proceeded to share the simple plans for the service, including a Bible reading of a few short verses, a sermon, and some reflections. He also added there would likely be a large turnout, and people would be able to speak briefly to share the cultural blessings Lucky had bestowed on them.

"It sounds a lot like our services in America," Christopher remarked.

Gavin nodded and then gently placed his hand on Christopher's shoulder to guide him through a back door into the church. "Would you sit with me in the service?"

Christopher smiled and nodded. "I would be honored."

After strolling down a long, narrow hallway, the two men ended up outside the rear entrance to the sanctuary. When Christopher slowly cracked the door open and peered in, he was taken aback at the sight of hundreds of people in attendance.

Gavin murmured, "Pretty astounding, huh?"

Christopher shook his head. "I don't know what to say. It's like Lucky was the local pope." He grinned.

Gavin shrugged. "Doesn't really surprise me. Lucky followed the divine principles very well, and as you learned, those principles are infallible. If you let them guide you, they will change you, other people, and, very likely, the world."

Christopher closed the door and spoke quietly to Gavin. "By the way, I'm the one who should thank *you* for letting me sit with you in the service. I know Lucky wasn't related to me, but in the short time I knew him, I felt like he *was* my family."

"Lucky would want it like this, Christopher. He didn't have any family—well, except for his daughter, whom he hasn't seen in years—and I believe you were like a son to him."

"It's almost like we were destined to meet—like we were *all* destined to meet." Christopher's glistening eyes led Gavin to pat him compassionately on the back.

A funeral home staff member approached the two and gently announced the service had begun. "You can enter with me, and I'll lead you to the front row, which is reserved for both of you."

With a deep breath, Christopher walked alongside Gavin into the massive sanctuary in front of the hushed congregation.

Once they were seated, the priest motioned for all attendees to follow suit. He welcomed everyone, shared an opening comment about Lou, and then proceeded to read verses which related to touching the world through love. After that, he began the sermon he had prepared, entitled "Impacting People's Lives Forever."

Just then, it occurred to Christopher that Lucky McGraw had gotten his wish.

He struggled to stem the flow of tears now engulfing him.

The sermon was powerful and poignant, and the congregation nodded nonstop at the speaker's accolades for Lou. Then as the priest finished, the congregants were invited to the front to share a personal memory of their dear friend.

The great space was still and quiet. But then, a dark-haired man, who appeared to be in his early twenties, stepped out from the very back of the crowd. As he slowly, quietly made his way forward, Christopher's eyes widened . . .

"*Sam!*" he breathed.

The barista had traveled across the world to see his friend off, and now he stood on the platform and began to speak.

"Lucky McGraw changed everything about my life. When I came to Lookout Mountain from Louisiana, I had nothing. I was a lost young man with a drug addiction. Lou saw through all of that and not only helped me get a job, but he also helped me get into college—something I never would have imagined possible for me."

After two more minutes, Sam dried his eyes and stepped down. He touched Christopher's shoulder tenderly as he walked by.

Again, there was silence.

Then, the next person made their way slowly down the aisle. This time it was a beautiful, dark-haired young woman.

Christopher's heart leapt. It was . . . *Madeline.*

As she reached the podium, her eyes caught Christopher's, and she abruptly looked away and began speaking. What she said shook the New Mexico man to the core.

She raised her eyes over the massive crowd and offered a sweeping gesture. "My father clearly made a difference in the world."

*Her father?* Christopher couldn't believe what he was hearing.

"To all of you, he was Lucky Lou McGraw. To me, he was . . . Daddy."

There was an eerie silence in the place as the young woman struggled to continue. "My name is Cara McGraw Stevens. When I was young, my dad was my everything—he was my best friend. He was always there for me. When I was with him, I felt I was in the presence of someone bigger than life itself, which I know now . . . he was."

Christopher leaned forward.

"Unfortunately, as time went on, we drifted apart, which I never saw coming."

She inhaled deeply and raised her chin.

"I stand here before you as a broken woman who wishes she could have understood things from his perspective. I wish I could do it all over. I wish I had known before that he loved me dearly . . . always. But I *didn't* understand, and I didn't give him a chance to tell me. I even changed my name from Cara to Madeline to make it harder for him to find me."

The woman reached into a small purse, then pulled out a tissue and began dabbing the corners of her eyes.

"My husband, Andy Stevens, died not too long ago, and his death caused me to realize how short life is for all of us. Even though I pulled away from my father for so many years, I began searching for him. When I heard he had moved to a little mountain town in the South, I was determined to find him and not only apologize, but *thank* him from the bottom of my heart—and hopefully start over."

Christopher's mind reeled as he thought of his own daughter . . .

"As luck would have it, I was within a mile—literally a mile—of finding my dad in Lookout Mountain. I couldn't muster the courage to go see him, so I kept going and going until I ended up in central Florida.

"One night in Tampa, I had a dream about needing to go back and find my daddy—no more excuses. I left the next morning, but when I got to Lookout Mountain, he had just left for Belfast. He never returned, and I was never given the chance to see him and make amends. I can only pray that he knows how I feel."

The sniffles of congregation members echoed throughout the large space as they acknowledged the deep pain of Lucky's daughter. Stepping off the platform, she walked dejectedly to the back and reclaimed her seat, head bowed.

After that, person after person came forward to share their stories of Lucky Lou McGraw. People from all over the world had come to pay their respects.

Some had received a visit from Lucky while serving time in prison. Others had been helped by Lucky after losing everything in a natural disaster. Still others who had been divorced, or who had suffered the death of someone close to them, spoke of how Lucky had made their lives more bearable.

When the last person left the pulpit over an hour and a half later, there was a profound stillness in the cathedral. In that moment, it occurred to Christopher that Lucky McGraw had lived the "luckiest" life possible.

In the days leading up to the service, he had wondered whether Lou's philosophy about a "carefully designed life of adherence to The Five Secrets" was nonsense after all. But today, Christopher realized Lucky Lou was right: a truly "lucky" person didn't win lotteries or find four-leaf clovers or have random good fortune, and they didn't have a bulletproof existence. They lived with faith and adhered to principles like St. Patrick's—and the result was a natural overflowing of blessings that *mattered*. Such a life had positive ripple effects for ages . . . long after the person was gone.

The priest asked everyone to stand, and as the Irish blessing "May the Road Rise to Meet You" was played softly on the piano, the congregation filed slowly out behind Gavin and Christopher. As they reached the back pew, Christopher paused and extended his hand toward Cara, who gratefully accepted the gesture, before stepping out ahead of the throng of well-wishers.

# Chapter Seventeen

Cara followed Gavin and Christopher back to the castle after the funeral. Once they arrived, the exhausted trio stepped inside, and Gavin introduced the young woman to Winston.

"A pleasure to meet you, Cara. You look so much like your father," he offered with a bow.

Her lips curved upward. "Thank you, Winston. I wish I had met you—and everyone else—a long time ago. But it wasn't meant to be, I suppose."

Christopher nodded his head in understanding. "He was an amazing man, and I was blessed to know him, even for a short period."

"Cara, why don't you stay for the night?" Gavin suggested. "I have a feeling you and I have a lot to talk about."

"You sure have a lot of explaining to do," Christopher added playfully.

She giggled and said, "I will—promise." Turning to Gavin, she added, "I'd like to hear as much about my dad as you can tell me. I've missed out on so much."

Christopher patted her shoulder. "It's strange how life happens, isn't it? You never know where your path will lead you. . . ."

Winston offered for the three of them to be seated in the living room for tea, which the group heartily accepted. Soon, they were chatting as if they had known each other forever, and the conversation went on for hours.

Finally, Cara glanced at her watch and realized how late it had gotten.

"It completely slipped my mind that all my things are at the hotel, so I guess I'll go back and spend the night there. It's not that far—I can come back tomorrow and join you both."

"I would love that," said Christopher, "but I'm going to let you two catch up on your own tomorrow—unfortunately, I need to head back to Lookout Mountain."

Cara tilted her head in surprise.

"I received a message from your father's housekeeper a little earlier. Apparently, he left something for me there. She couldn't elaborate, but it sounded like I should get going. My flight leaves in the morning."

Cara smiled and put her hands playfully on her hips. "You and I just keep missing each other, don't we? I'll be back in Lookout Mountain in a few days, and we can spend some time together there . . . if you're still willing."

Christopher chuckled. "We *are* long overdue for some pool time—plus, I owe you a thanks for the beautiful flowers you sent."

She flashed him another smile and then stood to leave.

Taking a subtle cue from Gavin, Winston offered, "William will gladly take you, ma'am."

Nodding, she turned toward Gavin and Christopher.

"Thank you for everything."

Christopher reached out and embraced her before stepping away so Gavin could do the same. They bid Cara good night in unison as Winston accompanied her to the car. With a crunch of gravel, the vehicle disappeared into the misty Irish darkness.

Christopher tossed and turned that night, waking up nearly every hour with thoughts of Lucky. He could hear his mentor's baritone voice of encouragement almost as if the Irishman was in the room.

When morning finally came, he headed downstairs, following the blissful smell of sausage and eggs. Gavin was already at the table, enjoying his coffee and reading the paper, when Christopher walked in. He folded back a page and turned it toward the American.

Gavin cracked, "I think Lucky would have liked that photo. Almost makes him look handsome."

"So, it was in the newspaper this morning? The obituary?"

"Not just the obituary. There are open letters from citizens, politicians, and business owners, all thanking Lou for what he did for them. It's astounding—here, take a look." Gavin handed the paper over to Christopher, whose eyes darted over it.

"Incredible."

Gavin nodded. "It's impressive, yes, but Lou trusted so deeply—it was all he knew . . . to trust and live out the secrets. His life was destined to impact many because of where his focus was—truly a lesson for us all."

*A lesson for us all* . . . The words seemed to echo through the room.

Christopher gently spoke. "My flight leaves in a few hours, Gavin. I'm going to miss you. My time with you and Lucky has changed me, and I'll always remember it."

Gavin smiled. "I've no doubt our paths will cross again. I'll send for William to bring the car around and help you with your luggage."

Christopher held up a hand. "No need—I appreciate you offering, but I've already arranged for a taxi so that William can be available for you or Cara if needed.

I'll just gather my things, and I'll be back down in a few moments."

Gavin put down his coffee and glanced out the window. "Of course. I'll be on the lookout for your taxi, then."

Christopher smiled, then strolled up the staircase one last time, scanning the castle and all its furnishings as if to lock it all in his memory. A few minutes later, he returned downstairs with his suitcase, and Winston carried it to the waiting taxi. Gavin stood at the open front door with his arms extended and embraced Christopher, who fully reciprocated the gesture.

As he pulled away, Gavin's eyes sparkled. "I have a feeling you'll be seeing much more of Cara. She seemed quite *smitten* with you, as I believe you say in America."

Christopher lifted his gaze to the sky, then back to his friend. "You know, I feel lucky enough to believe that now. Goodbye, my friend—and thank you."

Christopher stepped out to the waiting cab, shook Winston's hand firmly, and then slid into the backseat to begin the long journey home.

# Chapter Eighteen

The trip from Belfast to Chattanooga did not feel as long as Christopher thought it would be—probably since he slept most of the way. There was a short layover in New York where he grabbed a quick bite to eat, but he fell asleep again when he got on the next plane. He hadn't realized how exhausted the entire trip had made him until he stepped off the flight in Chattanooga and walked to the baggage claim.

He grabbed his luggage off the carousel, made his way to the taxi stand, then jumped into the first cab. A jovial, heavyset Indian driver hauled Christopher's suitcase into the vehicle, and they were off.

As the car exited the airport, the driver took a stab at small talk. "Lucky for you, the weather is so good today. We've had rain for five days straight!"

Christopher smiled and nodded. "Yes, I'm lucky like that."

The cabbie grinned and drove on, reaching Lou's house in just under half an hour. When they pulled into the driveway, Christopher cocked his head at the sight of two parked cars he didn't recognize.

*Hmmm, either Maggie got a couple of new rides, or there are guests.* He furrowed his brow and stepped out of the car, as did the driver.

"Whoa, whoa!" The cabbie threw up his hands when Lep came bounding out.

"He wouldn't hurt a flea," came Maggie's exasperated voice. She exchanged a smile with Christopher, though he could see the grief behind it.

"It's not fleas I'm worried about!" the man retorted nervously, his hands still raised.

Christopher laughed and reached out to pet Lep. The driver cautiously followed suit.

"Ah, he really is a sweetie," the relieved man said as the canine wagged his tail gently.

"He's the best." Christopher then reached in his pocket and pulled out a wad of twenty-dollar bills. "Thank you—and keep the change." He handed it to the smiling cabbie.

"My pleasure!" The driver turned and set Christopher's suitcase on the ground, then got into the car and slowly pulled off. About twenty yards away, he stuck his head out the open window and called loudly, "Love your place, sir!"

Christopher smiled, waved, and then turned to Maggie with a solemn countenance. "I'm so sorry about Lucky."

She wiped a tear away and said, "Yes, me too. About that . . ."

Christopher tilted his head.

"You have some guests inside. It's why I asked you to come back promptly. I apologize, but it's important business."

Christopher's brow creased. It didn't sound like good news, but he forced himself to remember The Five Secrets and decided to focus on potential success. *Wonder what good is going to come out of this?* he asked himself, plastering on a smile. He followed Maggie inside, Lep at his heels, and set his suitcase down by the front door.

Two men in suits stepped forward from the den. Both wore tortoise-rimmed glasses and were in their forties. One had short, brown hair, and the other had light blond hair—or, what was left of it.

The brown-haired man smiled faintly and stuck out his hand. "Hello, Mr. Stone. I'm Steven Krieger, and this is my partner, David Fine. We're from Heldman and Associates, and we represent Mr. McGraw and his estate."

Christopher turned to Maggie, whose lips curled up gently as she offered, "It's okay, you can trust them."

She motioned to the gentlemen. "If you'd all like to sit down, I'll bring out some coffee."

Still unsure, Christopher joined the two men as they seated themselves in club chairs around a coffee table in the den, Lep at their feet. David Fine opened a weathered brown briefcase and pulled out a stack of papers about an inch thick and plopped them on the table.

He began, "Mr. Stone, you're of course aware of Mr. McGraw's holdings."

"Um . . . should I be?"

The attorneys exchanged puzzled glances.

Steven Krieger explained, "Mr. McGraw had a net worth of approximately fifteen million dollars. He has ownership in several successful companies, plus a variety of land holdings, both here and in Northern Ireland."

"Okay . . ." Christopher stammered, "and what does that have to do with me?"

"Mr. Stone, he left most of it to you and his daughter—along with a tidy sum to Maggie."

Still reeling, Christopher breathed, "Are you serious?"

"Quite serious, sir. He also left you this home, which is worth approximately two million dollars."

With that, Mr. Fine placed two keys on the table—just like the pair Christopher remembered were once attached to the silver keychain.

"Oh yes, and all the contents of the house . . . including those in his wall safe, containing a certain"—Mr. Fine checked his notes—"historical scroll . . . ?"

Mr. Fine must have mistaken Christopher's look of shock for one of confirmation that he knew of the scroll, and concluded with, ". . . and of course, our client has made you guardian of Leprechaun."

Now thoroughly confused, Christopher sputtered, "What leprechaun?!"

A single bark cut through his thoughts, and he swiveled around at Lep.

"Oh!" he exclaimed, reaching down to pet Lucky's loyal canine, if only to buy time so that his thoughts could catch up with what he was hearing.

Christopher's eyes found Maggie's. "But, why would he . . ." His voice trailed off.

The lawyers shrugged. "No idea, sir," Mr. Krieger replied crisply.

The weary traveler palmed the back of his neck, still trying to take in what was happening. "What about Gavin?"

Maggie shook her head. "Mr. O'Grady decided it should be divided without him being involved. He and Lucky had specific conversations about that. As far as 'why you' . . . Lucky intuitively knew someone like you would come along, and in fact, he had been planning for it. He didn't know exactly when it would be or who, but he knew the right person to impact people's lives the way he wanted would show up."

She paused. "That person . . . *is you.*"

Christopher leaned back in the chair, laced his fingers together behind his head, and exhaled loudly.

Maggie added, "Oh, there is one more thing, Christopher . . ."

The New Mexican cocked his head in curiosity as she stood and walked toward an adjoining room. She tapped on the door and stepped back as it slowly opened.

The figure of a slender woman emerged, likely in her twenties, with long, golden hair.

"Hi, Daddy."

Christopher's knees trembled as he got to his feet, gawking with moist eyes. He inched closer toward her. "Megan, you're here. I . . . I can't believe it!"

The overwhelmed man wrapped his arms around her like only a father can, and the tears poured out.

Megan squeezed him tightly, and tears streamed down her face also. "Yes, it's me, Daddy." She laid her head tenderly on her father's chest. "I'm so sorry about all this time we've been apart. I'm never leaving you again, I promise. I can't tell you how much I've missed you. There were so many times I wanted to find you. I needed you, but it was all so confusing, and Mom . . ."

Christopher pulled back and shook his head to stop her as he wiped his eyes. "It doesn't matter. You're here now, and I couldn't be happier—I was so afraid I'd never see you again."

Right then, the attorneys stood up, preparing to leave.

"Mr. Stone, we'll be going now. Someone from our firm will reach out in a couple of days to iron out the details."

They took turns shaking the still bewildered man's hand, and then the two lawyers opened the door. Mr. Fine stepped out, and his partner followed him. As he started to shut the door, Mr. Krieger turned back with a hesitant look.

"Mr. Stone, may I say something?"

Christopher tilted his head and shrugged. "Of course."

"You're, well . . . you're one lucky man, sir."

The corners of Christopher's mouth turned up as he firmly clasped Megan's hand.

"Yes, you're right, Mr. Krieger. I am one *very* lucky man—and that's something I'll never, ever forget. . . ."

Find more of Skip's inspirational fiction and nonfiction books at

www.skipjohnsonauthor.com

# THE FIVE SECRETS OF LUCK

THE SECRET OF LUCKY WORDS

THE SECRET OF CONTENTMENT

THE SECRET OF SHARED LUCK

THE SECRET OF LUCKY PERSPECTIVE

THE SECRET OF LETTING GO

# MAY I ASK A FAVOR?

Thank you for reading my book! Would you do me a favor and take a moment to write a short review on Amazon? Reviews are extremely important to authors like me, and if you would share your thoughts so others can find out about my writing, I would be truly grateful.

If you leave a review, feel free to let me know by dropping me an email at skipjohnsonauthor1@gmail.com so I can personally thank you.

# Want To Get Weekly Inspiration From Me?

To get new, weekly inspirational stories and articles—and to stay updated on my release dates for new books—send an email request to me at skipjohnsonauthor1@gmail.com. I'll also send you an inspirational e-book of mine as a thank-you!

# About Skip Johnson

Skip Johnson is an award-winning inspirational author whose goal is to empower, inspire, and enrich the lives of his readers.

He is known for his easygoing style of adventurous storytelling, with rich elements of spirituality, mysticism, and personal growth woven throughout his books. One prominent aspect of Skip's writing is how he takes readers on symbolic journeys of self-discovery and enlightenment. His characters often find themselves on treks to faraway places where meetings with wise, mystical mentors lead readers to contemplate their own personal and spiritual journeys and how their lives can be more fulfilling and joyful.

Based in Georgia, Skip has traveled many paths, including that of a speaker, a business leader, a master tennis professional, and a world traveler. These experiences have shaped his writing, and the wisdom and insights woven into each story leave readers filled with wonder, gratitude, and enthusiasm for the days ahead.

In addition to *The Five Secrets of Luck*, Skip is the author of the novels *The Mystic's Gift, The Gentleman's*

*Journey, The Treasure in Antigua, The Lottery Winner's Greatest Ride, The Statue's Secret, The Cobbler of Cape Town, The Innkeeper's Journal,* and *The Gentle Warrior,* as well as the nonfiction books *Grateful for Everything, Hidden Jewels of Happiness,* and *Starting Each Day in a Powerful Way.* His works have earned The Maxy Awards Book of the Year, the International Book Award, and the Nautilus Silver Award. They have also been finalists in The Eric Hoffer Book Awards, The Feathered Quill Book Awards, and The Wishing Shelf Book Awards (UK).

www.ingramcontent.com/pod-product-compliance
Lightning Source LLC
La Vergne TN
LVHW051403080426
835508LV00022B/2945